Doggy
Business
101

A Practical Guide to Starting
and Running Your Own Business

Darlene Niemeyer

Doggy Business 101

Project Team
Editor: Heather Russell-Revesz
Copy Editor: Stephanie Fornino
Indexer: Lucie Haskins
Design: Stephanie Krautheim and Mary Ann Kahn

T.F.H. Publications
President/CEO: Glen S. Axelrod
Executive Vice President: Mark E. Johnson
Publisher: Christopher T. Reggio
Production Manager: Kathy Bontz

T.F.H. Publications, Inc.
One TFH Plaza
Third and Union Avenues
Neptune City, NJ 07753

Printed and bound in China
09 10 11 12 13 1 3 5 7 9 8 6 4 2

Library of Congress Cataloging-in-Publication Data
Niemeyer, Darlene.
  Doggy business 101 : a practical guide to starting and running your
own business / Darlene Niemeyer.
     p. cm.
  Includes index.
  ISBN 978-0-7938-0627-0 (alk. paper)
  1. Dog industry. 2. New business enterprises. I. Title.
  SF434.5N54 2009
  636.7068--dc22
                            2009015341

This book has been published with the intent to provide accurate and authoritative information in regard to the subject matter
within. While every reasonable precaution has been taken in preparation of this book, the author and publisher expressly
disclaim responsibility for any errors, omissions, or adverse effects arising from the use or application of the information
contained herein. The techniques and suggestions are used at the reader's discretion and are not to be considered a substitute
for veterinary care. If you suspect a medical problem consult your veterinarian.

The Leader in Responsible Animal Care for Over 50 Years!®
www.tfh.com

Contents

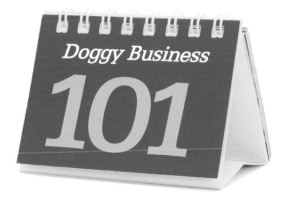

Introduction

Dog owners want the best care for their best friends. Our dogs provide us with comfort, companionship, and unconditional love. We, in turn, want to provide our dogs with the same level of care—especially when we must be away from them.

Because most dog owners work away from the home, they must leave their pooches early each morning (with guilt) and return home at nightfall (with guilt). This routine separation creates varying degrees of emotional discomfort for the typical dog owner. Today's working dog owners care for their pooches as much as they care for anybody in their lives. Dogs are now a part of the family, and as such, owners selectively invest in professional care for their dogs, just as they would for their children.

Unless someone stops by to feed and walk them and perhaps play with them, many dogs are left in a solitary world—lonely, bored, and yes, to a degree, neglected. There are more than 70 million dogs in the United States, and nearly half of these are left alone all day long.

With this emotional vacuum in a dog's life, there have been burgeoning businesses created to help solve the problem. These enterprises can benefit the dog, the dog owner, and the sensitive entrepreneur who starts and manages a dog care business.

Doggy Business 101 is intended to give novices as well as experienced business owners insight into the possibilities of exciting and lucrative dog-related enterprises. You'll discover new trends in comprehensive dog care and learn how to plan for, start, and operate your own dog business.

There's No Substitute

Dog owners try all sorts of techniques to give their dog some sense of companionship while away. They provide toys or stuffed animals or leave the television or radio playing to provide human voices and music for their dog to hear. But most owners come to find out that without some human (or another dog) socialization, these techniques can never replace having people or pets around.

Part I provides a detailed guide for anyone interested in starting a doggy day care business. Today, the fastest-growing dog-related business is the daily/weekly doggy day care. While the concept is relatively new, it's an exploding phenomenon across the United States and in Europe, with new facilities opening every month. They are becoming so popular that many entrepreneurs find that their facility is quickly filled to capacity and they must turn away new applicants.

Part II covers how to start up a dog sitting service or a dog walking service, plus takes a look at an up-and-coming business—dog camps. Dog sitting and dog walking services have been available for decades and used by millions of people. You'll find that what was once a casual hobby can be a lucrative and demanding enterprise.

Each chapter features a "Day in the Life" box with lessons learned from my own personal experience running a dog business. Plus, the Appendix and Resources contain sample business forms, documents, useful websites, and other sources to broaden your knowledge about these exciting and rewarding businesses.

This book serves as a comprehensive guide for starting a serious dog care business. It is intended to benefit the business operator, dog owners, and especially our dogs.

Why I Wrote This Book

After many years of caring for dogs after school, after work, and on weekends, I knew it was something I would enjoy doing on a full-time basis. I had done my share of dog sitting and dog walking and always felt comfortable caring for other people's dogs.

Although successful in my corporate career, there was something missing in the office environment. I missed caring for dogs and being around them, and I wanted to know what it would be like to start a business and make it a success. I looked into doggy day care centers and immediately thought that it was the perfect combination: a small business that would enable me to be with dogs all day long. I'd be making money doing what I loved!

Although I knew that I wanted to start this business, like so many people I initially lacked the guts to leave my corporate job. So I planned my steps—learning more about the business, saving money for the investment, and interviewing people with experience (including a consultant who understood the business). This took time, but as I learned more about the business process, I also learned more about me and my passion for dog care. I eventually came to the conclusion that I just had to try it. So I took the leap.

It was a nerve-wracking time. Not only was I breaking away from an interesting and lucrative career, a steady paycheck, and paid benefits, but I was starting a business most people had never heard about! It was scary to say the least. Even though I had done my homework (which gave me confidence), it took courage to move forward.

Like most business owners, I had my ups and downs in the beginning, but soon after the grand opening, my day care began taking off. Word of mouth about our loving care for the dogs rapidly increased our enrollment, and within months, the day care was profitable. Within one year I was at full capacity, with 50 dogs coming to the day care center daily.

There were long hours and many unanticipated challenges; there were surprises for me, for the dog owners, and sometimes for the dogs. But with dedication and a lot of perseverance, the center became a popular and respected business within the community.

After running that facility for more than three years, people from near and far began contacting me, asking how to create a doggy day care center and other types of pet businesses. I found that I enjoy guiding and helping others implement a business plan to start their own dog-related businesses. It reinforces my excitement and passion for establishing such wonderful services for dogs and their owners.

There are more than 72 million dogs in the United States, and more than five million puppies are born every year. One family in three owns a dog. That's a lot of clients from which to choose!

When I started, I had no idea there would be such an overwhelming response to my dog business and how rewarding it would be. I have since learned that this pattern is universal. Most well-run dog businesses are welcomed into the community, and the demand for such services is incredible.

Setting up and running your own doggy day care business takes time, patience, and proper research. These chapters will discuss the technical aspects of setting up and running a successful business.

Part I

Doggy Day Care Centers

However, anyone considering getting into the dog care field must keep the following in mind: Making the dogs happy and healthy should always be your first priority.

Why Doggy Day Care?

Let's explore what makes a good doggy day care center and find out if you are ready for this exciting and rewarding business.

What Is a Doggy Day Care Center?

Doggy day care centers (DDCs) are facilities that care for dogs when their owners can't be with them. Unlike kennels, where dogs are caged and boarded for extended periods, a DDC is a kennel-free environment where dogs play with other dogs and are supervised by professional dog care providers. The dogs socialize, play, eat, and relax in a safe environment. It is essentially a kennel alternative.

A doggy day care center is similar to a child's day care center, which provides affection, attention, playtime, and interaction with peers. And just like children's day care centers, the business owner must adhere to certain regulations and standards to maintain a clean, acceptable environment. In addition, the DDC must be closely monitored for safety. The professional staff needs to know how to supervise the various temperaments of dogs, watching for timid, aggressive, inattentive, and surly types. With their expert experience, they work with each dog to make sure that he is comfortable, safe, and happy.

Benefits of Doggy Day Care Centers

Up until the advent of the doggy day care center, dog owners who worked outside of the home had to leave their beloved pet unattended all day—anywhere from 8 to 15 hours. Some of these people hired dog sitters to come into the house for a short time to feed and walk their pooch. Although helpful, this type of service is limited and meets only the dog's most basic, functional needs. It does not include playing with other dogs, extended opportunities for romping around, or long periods of attention. With a DDC, however, dogs benefit in several ways.

Enforcing Good Business

I am actively in the process of drafting legislation that will improve the enforcement of dog care business requirements so that dogs are protected from less-than-sensitive business owners. These laws will ensure that dog care businesses always conform to good, healthy practices and will hopefully eliminate any businesses that might negligently treat our most beloved pets.

Socialization

To be well adjusted, dogs need to interact with other dogs on a routine basis, which is known as dog socialization. A DDC will inherently foster socialization skills. It helps acclimate dogs to playing and romping in a room with many other dogs. They meet dogs of their own breed, plus many other breeds. With proper supervision, the dogs naturally begin blending in with other dogs around them. After the novelty of being with many dogs at once has worn off, they become desensitized to the pack atmosphere. They begin to learn from the other dogs, acting less self-centered and more in unison with the dogs with whom they share time and space. (After all, dogs are pack animals.)

Without learning these essential socialization skills, some dogs end up barking, growling, or attacking strange canines on routine walks with their owners. But after enrolling in a DDC, dogs tend to become desensitized and are usually less reactive when encountering other dogs on walks in public parks.

At the DDC, dogs learn pack skills like playing, eating, drinking, and spending time together. They are forced to adopt less of a "me only" attitude and must learn to give and take with others, which makes for a more balanced dog.

Exercise

Doggy day care provides play and exercise for dogs, which keeps them alert, energetic, and physically fit. An owner who leaves her dog home all day is often greeted by an over-the-top, wiggling ball of energy that needs a good deal more exercise and playtime than she can give. With a DDC, when the dog and owner reunite at the end of the workday, both are tired and want to eat dinner, relax, and chill out after a full day of activity.

Less Stress

Owners who have their dogs enrolled in doggy day care centers have less stress in their lives. They don't experience the usual guilty feeling that they've neglected their dog during the day. Instead, there's relief knowing that he was entertained during the workday, playing and socializing with other dogs and the DDC staff. Some owners even become more focused and productive in their own jobs because those feelings of guilt and neglect go away after DDC enrollment.

Most centers open early in the morning and close in the early evening hours. This gives owners time to drop their pooch off early and drive to work. Likewise, they don't feel rushed on the return commute from work to get to their pet and rush him outside. Because there is always an attendant at the center, should highway traffic be delayed or if some other event prevents the pickup at the usual time, owners don't have to rush around in a craze trying to make it. Many DDCs offer boarding as well, so if owners need to leave their dogs for the night, they can do so knowing that their dogs are in good hands.

Doggy day care provides plenty of exercise for the dog.

Travel

Often when people want to take a vacation, they're unable to take their dog along with them. Rather than use the conventional boarding kennels, a DDC is a better alternative because it has supervised, unleashed playtime with the other dogs during the day. This is also true for the occasional trips away from home that everyone must take from time to time—a wedding, a reunion, a funeral, or a gala party, etc. It may only be for a weekend or a few days, but owners are more at ease knowing that a trusted and professional doggy day care center is available to care for their dog.

People are also starting to use DDCs as the vacation spot for their dog. They can check with their vacation destination or visit websites to learn if there is a DDC near their vacation spot. Then, while the family is at the beach, the slopes, or the amusement park, professional attendants care for the dog. The owners can later come to the DDC and take the dog out for a walk, a drive, or a romp in the local park. They can then drop the pup off during the evening, before they return to their own rental unit. It is a freer, more relaxed, and open option that has only recently become available. With this business model, the entire family can go on vacation together.

I happen to live in what is considered a seasonal resort area—Cape Cod, Massachusetts. We have millions of visitors here each year who want to bring their dog along for the vacation, but the hotel or rental agencies have historically prohibited pets from staying at the facility.

Fortunately, this policy is slowly changing. Many hotels and motels now have designated rooms for dogs to stay in with the family guests. The dog can be with his owners at night and dropped off at a local DDC during any outings where dogs might be prohibited.

If the dogs had up-to-date inoculation records and could pass temperament testing, we always welcomed doggy tourists into my day care center!

Remote Viewing

With today's advanced computer technology and high-speed communications, some centers offer computerized remote viewing. This means that the owner can watch her dog and his canine friends through a desktop computer via a webcam service. The webcam transmits in real time what the dog is doing. As the dog plays and interacts with other pooches and staff, the owner can observe. This way, the owner can still feel connected to her dog from the workstation at his office or even while he's on the road via a laptop. I offered this additional service at my DDC, and it was often the most attractive feature for the owners.

What Makes a Good Doggy Day Care Center?

If you are considering opening your own doggy day care center, you need to know what dog owners are looking for in a facility. Also, this is essential information for anyone looking to put her own dog into a DDC.

References

A good DDC has a list of customer references that potential clients can contact.

A prepared owner will find out about the facility's service, cleanliness, and overall impression through these references. She will sometimes ask if the customer's dog has had any changes in his personality or behavior since staying at the center.

It's a good idea to create goodwill with local veterinarians, groomers, and pet supply centers, as many potential clients may call them and ask about

Doggy day care centers come in handy for owners who must travel.

the facility. Because the well-being of dogs is foremost to these professionals, they will not be shy about passing on positive or negative experiences.

The Facility

A good DDC provides tours for potential clients and sets aside time for an interview. The guided tour should lead into all of the facility's areas, including the outside grounds for the dog.

Here's what potential clients look for:
- **Overall look of the facility**. It should have a logical organization. There should be adequate light, heat, cooling, and ventilation inside so that the dog is comfortable enough to play with others or nap when desired.
- **Cleanliness**. There should be no trash or unnecessary items strewn about.
- **Odor**. The facility should have a sanitized smell to it but not overpowering to dog or human.
- **Noise**. There should not be constant barking from every dog. The staff should have some control over the noise factor.
- **Supervision**. Staff members should be supervising the dogs and playfully interacting with them rather than just sitting around looking disinterested.
- **Size division**. There should be separators to keep large dogs away from the smaller ones.
- **Space**. There should be enough space to accommodate all of the dogs.
- **Safety**. The outdoor grounds should be safe from vehicular traffic. The fences need to be tall enough to prevent escape.

The Interview

The interview is probably the most critical step in convincing clients that a DDC is right for their dog. Any proprietor of a DDC should be well prepared to discuss the following questions or issues:
- How many buckets are filled with fresh drinking water?
- Is there an area designated for the dogs to lie down and nap?
- Are the large dogs separated from the smaller dogs with appropriate fences?
- Do staff members *constantly* supervise the dogs?
- What is the ratio of dogs to staff members?
- Are vaccination records required before enrollment?
- Is there an outside area for the dogs to relieve themselves? How often are they allowed outdoors?
- What are the hours of operation? Any days that the center is not open?
- Are there any billing discounts for frequent or continuous stays?

Neuter/Spay

Although neutering or spaying has no effect on personality overall, male dogs tend to display less aggression and territorial behavior when they are fixed. That is why it is imperative that dogs over the age of 6 months be neutered or spayed before continuing as a client in any day care.

- How are dogs disciplined for bad behavior? (e.g., time-out crates, spray bottles)
- Is webcam offered for remote viewing of the dogs?
- Is there an emergency escape plan in place?
- Is there a relationship with a local veterinarian?
- What is the maximum capacity of dogs in the facility at one time?
- What is the policy on food and snacks?
- What is the policy regarding unscheduled visits by the owner or her designee?
- How have the staff members been trained?
- How do staff members stop a dog fight from taking place?
- What do staff members do if there is an emergency with any dogs? Which vet is used if an emergency requires one?
- Do the staff members know how to perform CPR on a dog? Have they been certified on this procedure?

Be prepared to also answer administrative questions about insurance, billing, and payment options, and make available the operational policies/procedures brochure (if one is available).

Are You Ready?

The remaining chapters in Part I of this book will cover the steps, issues, and requirements for starting your own doggy day care center. But before we get to those topics, we must cover the hard and sometimes tedious task of determining the answer to this question: Are you ready to start a doggy day care business?

The key word here is *business*. This is not a trivial undertaking. Many people are not cut out to run a business. They have an unrealistic vision of what it will be like. It takes an unwavering

A good doggy day care has professional staff members who constantly supervise the dogs.

commitment and dedicated discipline to carry out business-related tasks on a scheduled basis. And let's not forget endurance! Some people might successfully start their own business and put it on the map, but after 6 or 12 months they burn out, get bored, or just lose the fire in their belly.

According to the U.S. Small Business Administration (SBA), nearly 85 percent of new small businesses fail within the first few years. The failure is not because the small business owner is incapable; it is usually caused by a lack of preparation and financial planning. Before you jump in to small business ownership with both feet, consider the following.

People skills are just as important as dog-handling skills when it comes to running a doggy day care.

Why Do You Want This Business?

Ask yourself why you want to run a dog day care business. What is your motivation? If the answer is simply "I really love dogs," or "I can't stand the boss I'm working for now and want to start something on my own," or "I just want to be my own boss," you may not be ready for such an undertaking. Many people love dogs, but will that love sustain in a multiple-dog environment for 365 days a year? Being your own boss may sound great, but are you truly ready to have the success or failure of a business rest entirely on your shoulders? Aspiring day care owners need a commitment and passion for taking care of all types of dogs and a clear understanding about the responsibility of operating a business.

Do You Have the Right Stuff?
What makes the right candidate to open a DDC?
Care History
Do you have a history of caring for dogs? You should be knowledgeable about caring for a pack of dogs, not just one or two at a time. Believe me, there is a huge difference!
Knowledge
It is very helpful to have some level of medical and technical knowledge about dogs and be able to identify problem temperaments and canine illnesses, as well as the corresponding remedies and protocols.

Understanding a Typical Day

Along with the capability to care for dogs, you should have a good basic understanding about what goes on in a DDC for 10 to 12 hours a day. You'll be keeping a vigilant eye on the dogs and occasionally be breaking up dog fights and disciplining dogs of all types.

Interpersonal Skills

In addition to qualifying as a doggy person, you're going to need good interpersonal skills with dog owners—in other words, you must be a people person. This is very important because most of your business interactions will be with dog owners and their wide array of personalities. You must deal with complaints and a multitude of personalities and attitudes. Keep in mind that your clients are only interested in their dogs—to an owner, her dog is the most important among all of the dogs enrolled in your program. The owner will often care very little about the other dogs. They want your focus to be on their dog as much as possible. Does this sound like a parent using a child day care center? You bet!

You must know what's going on in your DDC with every dog and be able to nimbly discuss any issues with the dog owner. This doesn't mean that you need to be submissive to the dog owner. On the contrary, you must be able to show strength and conviction—after all, you are the professional in this situation.

Just being a dog lover is not enough to make a DDC successful—you must understand the business as well.

The Good, the Bad, and the Ugly

Do you have a realistic perspective about running a DDC? If you are focused solely on the positive or rewarding parts of the endeavor, then you will be in for quite a shock about some of the daily (and more monotonous) aspects of running your own business. There are things you'll have to do, even if you don't like it.

As a day care owner you will be responsible for the dogs left in your care.

You should be prepared for "the good, the bad, and the ugly." Take some time to think about the following questions:

- Do you enjoy interacting with people just as much as dogs?
- Can you keep accurate records for billing and other required documentation for the business?
- Can you manage the paperwork for maintaining the operation?
- Can you handle the physical aspects of the DDC?
- Can you manage other staff members, including the hiring, disciplining, and perhaps firing of employees?
- Have you ever been in a managerial or supervisory capacity in the past? If not, imagine a few scenarios, such as having to fire an employee, and ask yourself how you would handle the situation.
- Do you fully understand the long hours and consecutive days that must take place at the facility—especially during times of illness, bad weather, staff absenteeism, etc?
- Are you willing to stay overnight if boarding is offered and special circumstances warrant your on-site presence?

Your Mandate

It's vitally important that you understand the real responsibility associated with the running of a DDC business. Think about the following: Dog owners are leaving you and your staff in charge of caring for what might very well be the most cherished thing in their life—their dog. These people not only expect but demand that their dog is always safe from harm. They are entrusting you to make sure that nothing negative happens to their dog while they are away. Any problems that happen at the DDC are ultimately your responsibility.

You must understand—truly understand—that you will be responsible for the care of many valued pets. They should always be your highest priority. If you are willing and able to work through the challenges and make sacrifices, then you are ready to continue planning this endeavor.

Now that you know that you are ready for this business, we can move forward and start the feasibility study.

A True Friend

Man can learn much from his dog, not only how to be a true and faithful friend but to appreciate those who love him.

A Day in the Life

One of my workers brought an unopened plastic bottle of diet soda into the day care. When the staff member left the room to get a mop to clean up a mess, one of the larger Labrador Retrievers decided to grab the full container of soda and play "keep-away" with the other dogs. While the dogs were running after the Lab with the plastic bottle hanging out of her mouth, the attendant ran in to take it away. Of course the Lab thought that it was a game and continued running! Suddenly her teeth punctured the plastic bottle, and we all know what happens to soda when it has been shaken—soda sprayed everywhere, startling all of the dogs. We gave a lot of free baths that day!

Lesson of the Day: Never allow attendants to bring anything into the day care. Inevitably, something will distract them and then it's open season on whatever was left behind.

Chapter

2

Feasibility Study

When I talk about a feasibility study, I mean testing and evaluating the probability of success with a comprehensive study of the proposed area of the business.

This phase of pre-business plan development is one that is often overlooked by entrepreneurs of all stripes. Most aspirants tend to jump right into the business plan without any thought given to how feasible it is for this enterprise to succeed in their geographic location.

Essentially, it is the feasibility study that determines if the business has a chance to make it in your area or neighborhood. But remember, this has to be done at the right time. It should always be done *prior* to developing a comprehensive business plan. Although many of the topics discussed here will seem to be obvious and self-evident, they are the basic issues that will make or break an aspiring business owner. In the case of opening up a doggy day care center, it is essential to answer these questions and issues before moving forward.

During the feasibility stage, you are exploring everything about a DDC but haven't made the commitment to begin—and you shouldn't until the full business plan is complete. But all of the tasks within the feasibility study build toward that goal. You can carry out the study while you still have your current day job, which will prevent you from jumping into this endeavor until the right time.

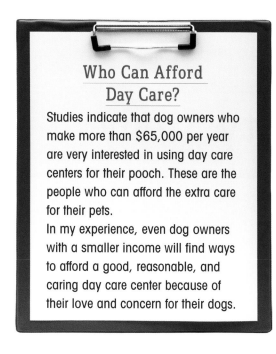

Who Can Afford Day Care?

Studies indicate that dog owners who make more than $65,000 per year are very interested in using day care centers for their pooch. These are the people who can afford the extra care for their pets.

In my experience, even dog owners with a smaller income will find ways to afford a good, reasonable, and caring day care center because of their love and concern for their dogs.

Determining the Need

Carefully and objectively consider the need. Is there a need for a service like yours in this area?

Where Do You Live?

If you live in remote, rural area with few dogs, and those owners keep their dogs with them all day, then we can assume that this is not a good place to start a DDC. If you are looking to start a DDC in an urban, suburban, or resort area, then the need for a facility is much more practical. These locations will have many dog owners who want dog care provided to meet their purposes.

Most urban and suburban areas will have a wide variety of breeds reflecting the wide variety of people who live there. These are prime potential areas to open a dog business.

The dog owners in these areas will usually have enough disposable income that the cost of these services is not an issue. In fact, recent surveys indicate that the cost of dog care is less of an issue with urban and suburban dog owners than it is with rural owners. Some studies indicate that these pet owners are willing to spend up to 10 percent of their income for professional quality dog care.

Are There Enough Dogs?

You need to discover if there is a considerable census of dogs living in your area. And if so, are they primarily indoor "house dogs" or large, guardian dogs who are kept mainly outdoors? Clearly, the former group is what you are looking to enroll in a DDC.

How do you learn more about the numbers of dogs in your targeted area? There are several methods.

Explore and Observe

The first method takes place on weekends and involves you exploring the area in which you are interested. As you walk, shop, or drive around town, take note of how many people are walking around with dogs. Observe how many dogs are in shopping mall parking lots waiting for their beloved master to return. During your observations, you can make assumptions about the neighborhood and the economic class of the residents. If it is middle to upper class, these dog owners will probably be interested in using a care center for their dog. Talk to anyone you see with dogs to learn of their interest.

Urban areas usually offer plenty of potential doggy day care clients.

Visit City Hall

The next stop to learn more about the local dog census is to visit the city hall in your area. Inquire about the number of active dog licenses registered with the town. This is public information, and if requested, they will provide you with a printout of all current dog owners and current licenses. (Obviously, you need to preface your inquiry as to why you want to know about the numbers.)

While you're at the municipal office inquiring about the dog census, you can also ask about opening up a new dog care business. Find out if the town requires any particular licenses for a DDC.

Veterinarians' Offices

Another place to visit is the local veterinarians' offices. Ideally, set up a meeting so that you can get each veterinarian's undivided attention. Explain the service you plan to provide, and ask for an approximate number of dogs for which the vet provides care. It also might be effective to take these professionals out to lunch to explain the purpose and goals of your DDC. It's an opportunity to underscore and convince the doctors and assistants that you have the dogs' best interests at heart.

The vet will also have a good idea of what percentage of her clients might be searching for a service like a doggy day care center. Ask questions about how the vet feels about a DDC coming into the area. This is a good time to schmooze and network with the vet. There are opportunities for you as a dog care provider and the veterinarian to collaborate on potential programs that can benefit everyone. Having the recommendation of local veterinarians is key and could quickly build up your business. (We'll discuss the marketing of your doggy day care center further in Chapter 8.)

Market Research Survey

By now you should know if the general population or census of dogs in your area is adequate to start a dog care business. You should also know intuitively if the dog owners are people who would be interested in daily dog care and be willing to pay for the service.

But there is one additional step you may want to consider during your feasibility study. It is optional and should only be necessary if you still have doubts about attracting enough customers to make your DDC work. You can prepare and distribute a "Market Research Survey." (See Appendix: Form 1 for sample.) Very simply, this is a one-page survey form asking dog owners if they might be interested in using a DDC for their dog. It can be done with just a few short, easy questions.

The survey should cover the following topics:
- A brief description of what services your DDC will provide.
- Their interest in doggy day care for their dog.
- Their interest in any additional services (grooming, training, etc.) at the facility.
- It's optional, but you can also ask for their name, the dog's name and breed, address, and phone numbers. (This will begin your marketing list for potential customers and will be helpful when you do your marketing and mailings.)

- Don't fall into a trap by asking how much they'd be willing to pay because the answers will sometimes be intentionally low and not accurate.

After your trip to city hall, you should have the names and addresses of many potential future clients. Mail the questionnaire to them, and for a better response rate, consider including a stamped return envelope.

You can also ask if the local dog supply store will keep your survey forms at their checkout counter. You can offer an incentive to customers to fill out the form by raffling off a gift card for the store, which you would purchase.

After you collect the forms, you'll have a clear indication if the interest in a DDC is high and sincere.

Finding the Right Location

The next part of the feasibility study is to determine possible locations. Location, location, location—it's been barked at every aspiring business owner for decades, but it still holds true. So many businesses fail not because of lack of capital or lack of hard work but because the location was all wrong.

Make it a point to meet with local veterinarians to discuss your potential business.

When establishing a doggy day care facility, there are several unique location factors different from the typical retail or service business. Many of these factors are interrelated and will also become the foundation for your business plan, which is discussed in the following chapter.

Municipal Zoning

You must first determine if there are any municipal zoning regulations for the business and square foot (m) area you are considering. For many areas, there are no specific regulations for DDCs, and in some cases, you might be directed to adhere to those rules outlined for dog kennels.

You should not be surprised if the DDC cannot be located in a residential area.

Operating a Doggy Day Care in Your Home

Although I don't think that running a DDC out of your home is the best business option, you may feel that you have no choice. If this is the case, there are certain things you'll need to be aware of.

- Every town has rules on what it considers the number of dogs to constitute a kennel. In my town, that number was four, which meant that I could legally watch four dogs in my home. Check with your town to find out the maximum number of dogs allowed.

- Your home must be safe. Dogs will put anything and everything in their mouths, so you'll need to puppy proof before you open your home to dogs. Decide if you are going to section off a certain area in which they are allowed or if they will have free roam of the house, and make those areas safe.

- You'll need an area where dogs can play outside and go to the bathroom. If you do not have a yard, you will need to walk them during the day. If you are unable to handle walking them all at once, you'll have to walk them a few at a time. In this case, you must have someone watching the others while you are gone. The dogs must never be left alone…ever!

- Make sure that your fencing is strong and high enough to discourage any jumpers. The dogs shouldn't be able to dig under the fence either.

- Always ensure that your yard is clean of feces. As gross as it sounds, the dogs will eat them, which can cause severe sickness.

- The dogs' shots must be up to date—kennel cough included.

- Cleanliness is imperative—germs spread quickly.

- Create a separate area for feeding the dogs individually. Food aggression can turn the nicest dogs into crazed animals.

- You'll need an area for time-outs for dogs who can't calm down.

- Set rules for your daycare as if it were a full-blown operation—all of the things we discuss about running a larger operation should be followed in a home day care.

Think carefully before running this business out of your home, and if you do decide to go ahead, follow the law and don't take on too many dogs just to make some quick money.

Zoning

Your trip to city hall is also an opportunity to discover any zoning ordinances that are on the books. Make a copy of the requirements, as they'll come in handy when you are identifying and selecting locations and buildings that might be useful. Also inquire if you must formally present to a zoning board or committee your proposed plans for such a dog care business in your municipality. Ask if there will be a town inspector who will visit your facility before you open your business. (Be prepared for inspectors to visit, including electricians, building department officials, fire marshals, etc., during all phases of development.) This planning is essential for the smooth and successful implementation of your DDC. The town can and will shut you down in a minute if everything is not up to code.

While there are some doggy day care centers located within residential areas, they are small, have only a few dogs, and are only marginally larger than a dog sitting business. (See box "Operating a Doggy Day Care in Your Home" for more information.)

Even if it is possible to run a DDC in a residential neighborhood, it's hard for me to fully recommend it. To be successful, people need to support your business. Nearby neighbors are not likely to want 50 dogs in one building on their block! The noise factor alone would ensure unhappy neighbors.

Transitional Zone

If local commercial zones or popular shopping malls do not accept your type of dog care business, you must look outside the inner city's hub. But this location need not be out of the way in outlying remote sections of the town. Most towns and their zoning policies have what is generally known as a "transitional zone." While this is not a residential area, it's also not way out on the outskirts of town where heavy industrial companies are typically in operation.

Transitional zones typically sit between the commercial hub of the town and those remote locations with heavy industrial operations. They are often populated with small commercial enterprises, light manufacturing, and small warehousing. They usually have minimal pedestrian and vehicular traffic. They're often characterized by wholesale storage facilities, distribution centers, and light, nonoffensive industries. Fortunately, they are usually close to a primary or secondary highway network, which is critical for your DDC. It must be easily accessible from major roads because your customers will be commuting to their workplace each day via the highways.

Transitional zones may actually be preferable to shopping plazas, where the dogs would need to be walked by hand because most shopping malls wouldn't have a place for the dogs to go to the bathroom.

Determining the Space

Your DDC will need a play area for the dogs. The usual guideline is minimally 70 square feet (21 sq m) per dog for the play area. For larger dogs, this space requirement becomes even bigger. So if you plan to house about 40 dogs at capacity, you will need at least 2,800 square feet (853 sq m) of play area in the building. In addition to that, you will need space for a reception area, various storage areas, and a bathroom. If you anticipate having additional services at your DDC (grooming and boarding), you must allocate the appropriate space. (Chapter 5 includes a detailed discussion of design and layout of a DDC.)

Adequate Parking

Your facility must also have an adequate short-term parking area. Remember, your customers will drive to your DDC each morning to drop their pup off and then return in the early evening to pick him up. Most of your customers who work a 9-to-5 job will be coming to your place around the same time. You don't want them to end up frustrated with little or no parking space.

The parking area should also be paved. No one likes stepping into muddy puddles (except, perhaps, for some dogs!).

Sketch Out a Floor Plan

If you find a facility, such as a warehouse or abandoned factory building, sketch out an existing floor plan while you are there. Then when you get home, you can try different layouts to give you the space requirements mentioned earlier to see if the building will work for you. You can make it pretty later—for now, you're just trying to identify the essential elements of the DDC layout.

Expansion Possibilities

If you start small with your DDC, you'll want to find a place that has room for expansion. Many day care centers start with a small building with a limit of perhaps 20 to 25 dogs. They often reach their capacity in just a few months and end up turning cash-paying dog owners away. This is something you want to avoid.

Select a site that is expandable, or find another site nearby to accommodate a waiting list. The former is preferable because you need only add minimally to your equipment,

Parking Lot Tip

When you are running your DDC, make sure that checking the parking lot for dog feces and hosing it down becomes a routine daily task. Nothing will upset your cash-paying dog owner quicker than stepping in a pile of dog poop! (It happens, believe me.) If at all possible, try to set up a small area outside where dogs can be walked for elimination purposes before coming in. This will keep the soiled area contained, making daily cleanup easier.

Shopping malls may not be the best fit for your doggy day care, as there is often nowhere convenient to let the dogs play outside.

space, and staff. If not, it is important to find a new location that is not too far away from your original site. This will prevent your customers from being inconvenienced.

Finding the Right Building

Once you become familiar with the business zones and corresponding regulations around your town, you must identify a building that you can rent or buy, then renovate and improve to build your DDC business.

Visit a Working DDC

Before finding a building, you must know what is minimally required within the four walls of the DDC. There aren't many ways to quickly learn about this important aspect of the business because the concept is fairly new. The best way is to contact someone who is running this type of business and ask permission to do a site visit. Ideally, it will be within an easy traveling distance, simply because you may want to check out the operational DDC facility more than once. (If it is not possible to find a DDC to visit, seek a consultant who has either run a DDC or has knowledge about operating one.)

When you visit the DDC, remember that you now must look at the space, heating, plumbing, cooling, and ventilation as a potential owner and not as a user. You must look at the entire infrastructure, including water supplies, hose faucets, storage, lighting, and everything that makes this not only an appealing and effective facility but that also conforms to town regulations for a DDC.

While nothing compares to seeing an operating DDC for yourself, here are some of the minimal requirements your building will need:

You may get lucky and find a building that meets many of your needs—this way, you won't have to spend as much on the build out.

- water supply
- plumbing
- heating and cooling system
- storage
- electricity
- sewer line
- two doors
- handicap access
- drainage inside to hose the floors down (bonus but not necessary)
- ability to section off different areas—lobby, office, day care area, grooming, boarding
- anything else that that town regulations require for the business

Looking for a Building

First, try driving around on your own to look for any buildings that might qualify, noting if they are vacant or might be soon. If you find one, you can contact the owner directly and meet to discuss opportunities. You may find some landlords to be less than open to this type of business, but don't let that stop you. Be prepared to go over all of your plans and convince them that you know what you are doing.

If you cannot locate a building on your own, contact a commercial real estate broker, who will negotiate on your behalf. Brokers usually have many more opportunities to find the right location for your facility.

Visiting Potential Sites

If you find a building that may meet your requirements, it's time to do a site visit. You should prepare a very general concept of your design and bring it with you. (You will be continually updating your preliminary design.) Hopefully, you've been able to visit multiple day cares in person and have found some ideas online for your own concept. Of course, every day care will mimic the individual owner's tastes, but it's good to have a basic idea of what you want.

Also, it is often wise to bring a building contractor with you so that you can have another pair of expert eyes to investigate the potential site. The contractor will know more about building structure and can inspect the pipes, heating/cooling source, and other construction issues you may not feel comfortable evaluating.

Pros and Cons of Storage Sites

You might find a structure that is ideal in location, space, and accessibility. But if the building was used only for cold, dry storage, it will require some work. It will need a water supply connected to the water main. It will need heating and cooling and insulation for the required comfort of the dogs and staff. Additionally, it will need sewage connectivity, air handling systems, electricity, and of course, internal plumbing.

Also, there should minimally be two doors to the building, which is not always the case with storage facilities. Now that the facility will be housing humans and many valuable dogs, these lives must be protected in case of immediate evacuation. Fire and emergency safety issues that were not a problem when the building was used only for storage must be addressed. I bring these potential problems up because so many people become enamored with the low cost of leasing such a building without thinking fully about the build-out features that must be added—and paid for.

One plus to storage or warehouse sites is that their owners are often anxious to have a tenant, which means that they are usually more flexible than most landlords when it comes to making structural changes to the building. For instance, boarding up windows, adding exposed water piping, sinks, and other changes are usually more acceptable to a warehouse owner than a retail store landlord.

Modifying a storage site may be a good option as a potential doggy day care facility.

Any renovations you can do yourself will help save you money—even something as simple as painting.

Modifying the Building

If the building you have in mind is going to be a lease arrangement, you must find out if you can modify the structure. Generally, these modifications will be internal and cosmetic and don't affect the foundation or structure. If modifications are allowed, you can then estimate what your annualized rent with the required capital for building out will be (i.e., your rent plus the cost of renovations).

Getting Estimates

If modifying the building is necessary, you will need to hire a general contractor or various electricians, carpenters, plumbers, and painters to convert the building into your perfect DDC. Meet with these tradespeople and tell them what you need, and then get an estimate from them. These estimates are input to your business plan. (See Chapter 3.)

Do It Yourself

It's helpful if you are able to do some of the renovations yourself. To save money, owners should do as much of the less technical work— such as painting and decorating—as possible. Painting may not seem very important, but you want your day care center aesthetically pleasing for the dog owners (although the dogs don't much care). Many DDCs have colorful murals painted on the walls with trees, blue skies, dogs, toys, etc. It makes for a more pleasant environment and creates a sense of peace in what is usually a raucous and highly energized setting. Plan for the things you must contract out and which tasks you can get done with you and your friends working together.

Meeting Potential Neighbors

Once you have a signed lease on a building, it's extremely beneficial to take the time to introduce yourself to the business owners of the abutting and nearby buildings. They'll get to know you as a person, which is always nice, and it gives you an opportunity to explain your business and how you intend to operate it. You can reassure them that there won't be a negative impact on their respective businesses. Visiting the neighbors also stems any negative or malicious rumors about what might be coming into the area. It always helps to keep people informed, and your new neighbors are no exception. Encourage them to come to you with any issues or complaints if they arise so that you can resolve them as quickly as possible.

Building It From Scratch

If you have the capital to build a brand-new facility for a DDC from the ground up, then by all means go for it! You will still need to know the exact design and layout of your center. However, in this case you should also hire an architect and a commercial contractor to build the facility exactly the way you want the structure to be built.

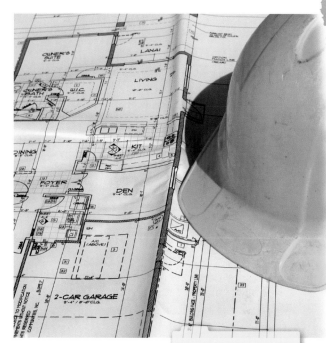

If you have enough capital to build your facility from scratch, go for it!

Before you do this, visualize the look and feel of the center. Is it going to be wide open, or will it be compartmentalized? Will you be offering bathing and grooming services? Will you be offering overnight boarding? Do you want an employee lounge to escape the happy hounds from time to time? Do you want a retail store or section to sell popular doggy items? Retail is a great way to make extra money, and you have a captive audience! Have all of your ideas reviewed by a current DDC owner or a knowledgeable consultant before going forward.

There are distinct advantages to building your own facility. You can design the structure to be expandable. So if your initial goal is to have a 40-dog capacity, later you might want to expand with an addition or second mini-facility to bring the daily enrollment even higher.

However, besides the higher cost, there's another disadvantage to building the facility yourself—the inevitable delays in finishing the project because you'll need to work with the town during each phase of build out. It will never go quite as quickly as you predict.

Finding Competent Staff

You need to ascertain the availability of staff for your DDC in the feasibility stage. If you jump into this business without competent staff to help you, you'll have a very rocky beginning—or even face failure. Without good staff, you'll have potential safety issues with the dogs, which is a surefire way to fail at your dog care business.

Here's what you need to know: Are there qualified, responsible, and reliable people who will help you operate the facility? Are they experienced in working with dogs of all sizes and shapes? Are they strong enough to discipline and handle misbehaving dogs? Do they have the patience and endurance to put in long hours and sequential days performing

You'll need to determine if adequate staff is available in the area in which you are interested.

this job? And lastly, if there are qualified candidates, what salary or hourly wage will they be looking for?

To help answer these questions, develop a list of potential employees as you gather your information during the feasibility study. By now you have started to get the word out about your DDC, and people may approach you for prospective hiring. You've also informed the town hall, the pet stores, and some vets about your enterprise, and they could supply you with names of people who might be eligible to work in your dog care center. Using this list, call potential staff to find out a little about their backgrounds, and also use this as an opportunity to learn what their hourly wage requirements might be. This exercise should also take into consideration optional benefits for your full-time employees. These offerings translate into a line-item expense when you develop the business plan.

How many employees will you need? The general rule is 1 staff member per 10 dogs. This can be adjusted depending on the needs of the day. It's always wise to plan on several part-time positions for your weekly coverage so that you have staff that can adjust their work hours and fill in when emergencies arise.

Purchasing a Franchise

The franchising of doggy day care centers is another option now catching on. As of this writing, some of the larger pet food/supply markets are offering DDC franchises. Like with any franchise, you are not the true owner; you simply manage the business to earn your portion of the profits. You will not have the latitude to make structural changes within the facility, with the policies, or in the daily operation.

It is often difficult to satisfy a personal passion and dream with the franchising model. But the risks are much fewer. If you would rather not go through the hassle of building your own center and prefer a more structured approach, then a franchise may be perfect for you. Keep in mind that franchising can run you as much—if not more—money than starting your own. But a major advantage with franchising is that you can amortize your buy-in over a period of several years, which means that you won't need as much money up front and can avoid some of the bureaucratic and administrative headaches that loans from commercial banks require.

The feasibility study broadens your knowledge of what you must do long before you put the key in the lock to open the door on your grand opening day! You now know if opening up a DDC is feasible in your area; if there are potential dog owners who will become your loyal customers; and you have a general estimate as to building costs. Now you can see why this phase is so important. Feasibility planning is a critical keystone for the next phase: developing your DDC business plan.

A Day in the Life

A German Shepherd Dog applied for my day care who did well integrating with the other dogs but couldn't be kept in a crate because he always managed to escape. The owners told us up front about this challenge, so with some reservations I decided to accept the dog into the day care program but not accept him for boarding. One Saturday night the owners couldn't pick up their dog due to an unforeseen emergency. Although I wasn't thrilled, I had no choice but to board him overnight. I placed that dog in our most secure crate, then turned it around so that the door of the crate was facing the wall. I felt confident that he couldn't escape when we locked up for the evening. (By the way, Saturday was our "extreme cleaning day," and the day care was in tip-top shape when I left.)

The next morning, as my manager and I pulled up to the center, we noticed the big Shepherd's head staring at us from the office window—not a good sign. As we opened the door, we couldn't believe our eyes—the office was trashed beyond description. Every plant was ripped apart and tipped over, the floor was shredded, the door handle appeared to have been chewed on all night…the list of damages went on and on. I didn't know one dog could do so much harm!

Lesson of the Day: Stick to your guns when it comes to what dogs you accept into your DDC. Don't bend the rules, and always go with your gut instinct!

Chapter

3

Developing a Business Plan

Many people cringe at the thought of developing a business plan, but it is the preparation of this vital document that can ensure success for any new business.

The idea of creating a business plan may seem tedious or even threatening, and I often hear negative statements like "I'm not good with numbers," or "I never took an accounting class, so creating a business plan isn't for me," or "I know dogs and how to care for them, so what do I need a business plan for?" But creating a business plan is essential for any start-up business. Banks or lending institutions will not entertain a small business loan if there is no business plan—it is the one document that lenders require. They will study and evaluate it for accuracy before bringing a loan request to committee. It also proves to the lender that you've done your homework.

We've already helped alleviate most of the tediousness thanks to the feasibility plan from the previous chapter. And after you read this chapter, you'll realize that there is certainly no need to be an expert in accounting to create a comprehensive business plan.

You should be working on your business plan constantly.

What Is a Business Plan?

In the simplest terms, a business plan is a financial tool to manage a business. At the core of most business plans is an accounting spreadsheet called a "Profit and Loss Statement," which is usually split up into two major sections: projections of monthly income and projections of monthly expenses. Here, the word "projection" means much more than just an "educated guess." A projection can only be derived after you have done your research during the feasibility stage, including the building and its modification costs, the staff, the prospective clients, and associated expenses and revenue. If you've done your research correctly, your projections will be accurate and your plan will succeed—and so will you.

The task of creating a business plan is not done quickly in one night while sitting in front of the television. If you are truly passionate about becoming a successful DDC owner, you should be thinking about it most of your waking hours. It's something that you should take with you as you go about your daily activities. As a thought comes up, you can take out your plan and annotate it to reflect any relevant changes in costs and income. You may find it helpful to carry a mini-recorder with you so that when ideas come up, you can record them for later review. Often, minor expenses are overlooked when you form your business plan, but they can add up quickly and make or break your business.

What most people don't understand is that the business plan is not something that's thrown together, printed, and then discarded after grand opening day. The business plan is not a one-shot deal; it's a dynamic progress report. You'll be monitoring it after your business starts and then checking it after each month, after each quarter, and year after year. If done properly, it will help guide you in budgeting, managing, enhancing, and expanding your DDC.

Getting Help With the Plan

There are entire books dedicated just to the topic of creating a business plan. This chapter is meant to give you a basic frame for your plan and address some specific DDC needs. But you should also consult with other resources that can help you with some of the details of the plan that we don't have room for in this book. The most accessible resource is the Internet, as there are many websites that offer excellent information and even spreadsheet templates for developing business plans.

One of the most useful resources I've come across is the Service Corps of Retired Executives (SCORE). Created under the wing of the U.S. Small Business Administration (SBA), SCORE comprises local organizations of professional counselors who help small business owners get started or enhance their established operations. There are more than 350 SCORE chapters throughout the United States.

The SCORE counselors offer many kinds of business advice, but their specific forte is to help individuals develop their initial business plan. And the best part? All of this advice and counseling is *free*!

When you approach your local SCORE office, don't be anxious about not knowing business planning procedures. The counselors have a wide background of experience and will walk you through the steps of setting up your plan so that you feel comfortable and confident. They will show you how to outline your new business so that you can seek and receive capital funding to start it up. And they'll continue to follow up with you after your doggy day care center is in operation—all at no charge to you.

In addition to the counseling sessions, SCORE offers a small business planning educational program. This program is usually offered twice a year and will introduce you to small business terms and techniques to start up any business in your particular area. There is usually a small fee to take the eight-week course.

I strongly encourage you to use this professional service. You just need to call to make an appointment and show up. The counselors will guide you through the steps to developing a successful business plan and get you started following your dream.

Starting a Small Business

There are several places on the web you can visit to find out more about starting a small business, including:

- SCORE (www.score.org)
- About.com's Small Business Information (http://sbinformation.about.com)
- Entrepreneur (www.entrepreneur.com)

Business Plan Content

Although business plan formats may vary, the most important thing is the content. It is what you will present to potential funding sources and should be as comprehensive as possible. It is crucial that you present your material in the most complete and accurate light possible. Banks, lending institutions, and potential investors have a higher regard for the small business owner who takes the venture seriously and puts her best effort into everything. A document that is complete and professionally presented will be a positive factor in seeking business loans. SCORE's website has many useful templates that can help make developing your business plan easy.

Your business plan should be as comprehensive as possible.

Section 1: The Business and Its Scope

Section 1 of the business plan is an overview of your doggy day care business. It should include the following:

- description of a doggy day care center
- business name and mission statement
- estimated opening date
- location
- list of services
- rates
- hours of operation
- your position in the business

Description of a Doggy Day Care Center

Describe what a DDC is—this is important because the concept may still be new to some people.

Business Name and Mission Statement

You'll need to get your creative juices flowing and come up with a name and mission statement for your doggy day care center. Hopefully, you've been thinking about potential names and have a few options in mind.

Naming Your DDC

Naming a business is tricky, but at the same time, it can be fun. The first thing to do is search to see if the name you want is being used by another business in your state and/or country. You can check this out online, and there are databases of named businesses already active in your area. Depending on the level of protection they have set in place (such as a copyright), you'll need to avoid using the same name. Be aware that many databases are not real time and can be outdated—many are up to almost two years old.

The next thing to consider for your business name is branding. You're going to want to associate it with everything you do—maybe even develop your own products down the line—so you need to make sure that the name you choose can work for many purposes. Come up with a tagline and logo as well. The idea is for potential customers to remember you whether they hear the business name, see the logo, or hear the tagline. So let's say that you've decided on the name "Four Legs Good" for your DDC. Your tagline could say something to the effect "Where Your Dog is Always in Good Hands." And your logo could have some fun art incorporated into it. For example:

Four Legs GoodDog Day Care
Where Your Dog Is Always In Good Hands

There are plenty of words for "dog," so get creative! If you can't think of anything, hire a designer to help you come up with a good name and logo. Or have a party at your house with friends and make a game of it—you'd be surprised how well this works.

The table on page 44 provides you with a list of dog-related words that you can mix and match to get your creative juices flowing!

Dog Business Name Finder

Paws	Pooch	Poochie	Pets	Resort
Salon	Camp	Muddy	Canine	Pals
Tails	Happy	Friends	Critters	Kingdom
K9	Pups	Doggy	Four legs	Diva
Paradise	Retreat	Club	Rawhide	Stud
Four stars	Getaway	Palace	Spa	Hydrant
Run	Hound	Kisses	B&B	Dawg's
Barkers	Wag	Tails	Furry	Homedog

Remember, make it catchy and fun!

Once you have decided on the name for your new venture, it's a good idea to put some protection on it in the way of a trademark or copyright mark. After all, you don't want anyone stealing your ideas.

Mission Statement

A mission statement explains the priorities, values, and intentions of your business. Once your DDC is up and running, it will serve as a guide to help you stay focused on what is important.

For example, your mission statement could read something like:

Our mission at "Four Legs Good Day Care" is to provide a safe, loving, and fun environment for dogs. We want to be the number-one dog care provider of choice, and will provide our clients with peace of mind, knowing that they are leaving their dogs in the best of hands. We promise that your dog will receive all the love and attention he needs, and we'll be your dog's home away from home.

You can add your mission statement to your brochure, website, or other marketing materials. The mission statement can be changed as you grow your business.

Estimated Opening Date

You can get a general idea of your opening date from the contractors, but realize that it is not set in stone. (You might want to think about offering an incentive for the contractor to finish on time. It's something I wish I had thought of with my own DDC, which was supposed to open in the month of November but it didn't happen until three months later—it was a lot of carrying costs that I had not factored in.)

Location

List the address and a crossroad or a focal point (e.g., "next to the Home Depot" or "in XYZ Plaza.") You may want to even include directions coming from north and south.

List of Services

List all of the services you will offer, including day care for dogs, overnight and weekend boarding, grooming, training, retail store, etc.

Rates

Your feasibility study should have provided information on what a typical DDC charges for daily, weekly, and monthly day care. DDCs in highly populated suburban areas usually charge more than those in remote areas.

You should have a set rate for a half day and a higher rate for a full day. Think about offering sliding scale rates for clients who are permanent enrollees or discounts for multiple dogs. Offer a discount for anyone who uses your DDC daily—you can get creative and have "club" memberships or offer punch cards. For a sample "Hours of Operation and Rates," see Appendix: Form 2.

> If you've done your feasibility study correctly, your business plan will be much easier to put together.

Hours of Operation

You'll want to list your intended hours of operation. Because most of your clients will need to drop off their dogs before work and pick them up afterward, you'll need to factor those times into determining your hours. If you live in a rural area where traveling time is not as hectic, you can probably close a bit earlier than a more suburban or urban area. You may also want to open later and close earlier on the weekends. For example, my own hours of operation were Monday through Friday, 7:00 a.m. to 6:00 p.m., and 8:00 a.m. to 5:00 p.m. on weekends. For a sample "Hours of Operation and Rates," see Appendix: Form 2.

Raising Rates

Don't underestimate your service rates in the beginning with the intention of raising them after your clientele expands. It's a pitfall I made and came to regret. Raising rates for your charter members within months after opening is not a good idea because they will resent it, and you'll lose business. It is better to establish your rates a little higher in the beginning and keep them at the same level for a year or longer.

Your Position in the Business

Explain what your position in the business will be. Most likely you'll be running the day-to-day operations, with the eventual goal of working "on" your business and not "in" your business.

Section 2: Market Analysis

Section 2 is a narrative summary of your feasibility study research. It should contain:

- why a DDC will work in your area
- why a DDC is needed
- competition

Why a DDC Will Work in the Area

Explain the research you did in the feasibility study. This summary should contain your observations of what's going on in the area, what the population is like, and the people who will need the service.

Why a DDC Is Needed

Summarize why a DDC is needed in your intended location. This information should be readily apparent to you if you've done the feasibility study correctly.

Competition

Describe the other established pet-related services in your community and explain how you would complement/compete with them.

The financial data you provide in your business plan will help assure loan officers that your business will be profitable.

Section 3: Management and Personnel

Section 3 covers the team of people that will help your DDC succeed. It includes:

- owner/operator
- assistant manager
- other staff
- independent contractors
- team of advisors

Owner/Operator

List your bio, resume, and why you are qualified for this undertaking.

Assistant Manager

If you intend to hire an assistant manager right away, put in a job description of this role. If you happen to already have someone in mind who is interested in the position, you can add that person's name.

Other Staff

List the number of full-time and part-time staff you will need. A good estimate is one staff member for every seven dogs. That being said, you could have ten very mellow dogs and one person would be enough. You'll make staffing decisions as you start running the business, but the 1 to 7 ratio is a good safe place to start for your business plan.

Independent Contractors

If you plan to allow a trainer or groomer to work out of your facility, list her here.

Team of Advisors

List the team of advisors you will rely on to help start and run your business. They will include:

- accountant and/or bookkeeper
- attorney
- consultant and/or advisors (e.g., SCORE)

List their names and addresses. This information is basically to show that you've done your homework and are taking into consideration every aspect of the business.

Section 4: Financial Information

This section deals with the financials of your DDC. Some of this is descriptive information, and some includes the data that you'll enter onto spreadsheets. What I'm outlining here are the basics—you certainly can (and should) get more detailed with this information.

Start-Up Costs

Create a spreadsheet that will detail the expenses involved in starting your DDC. Create a line item for everything you'll need to spend money on for your start-up. This can include:

- remodeling of facility
- rent deposits
- utility deposits
- first few months' operation for payroll, rent, etc.
- insurance
- advertising plan and its costs (see Chapter 8 for more information)
- website development and maintenance costs
- legal and professional fees
- supplies, including day care items and office supplies (for a complete list, see Chapter 5)
- inventory, including start-up retail inventory and working inventory (for a complete list, see Chapter 5)

Research the estimated costs for each item and add them to your spreadsheet.

Tax ID

If you choose to sell retail items at your DDC, get a sales tax ID number from your state's department of revenue. With this tax exempt number, you can purchase items at wholesale prices without paying sales tax and then sell them at a profit at the retail price you set.

Facing Reality

Some small businesses don't make it, even though they've completed a business plan. This is usually due to coming up with inaccurate figures. Potential business owners can overlook or underestimate expense items or overestimate revenue stream. This often happens because they didn't want to face the harsh reality of the business side of a DDC. They were too anxious to get going and to start the business. They led with their hearts and not with their heads. Make sure that the numbers you are estimating are coming from reality, not wishful thinking.

Capital

On your start-up spreadsheet, list all of your sources of capital as line items, including:
- the amount of capital you are able to contribute
- any additional capital funds you will be receiving from friends, relatives, venture capitalists, etc.
- bank loans

After you take into account the amount of capital you have, the loan you will need is the difference between your capital and the start-up and short-term running costs of your DDC.

Profit and Loss Statement

The profit and loss statement should be the centerpiece of your business plan. It is not only necessary to show loan officers and potential investors, but it's the piece of the puzzle that will tell you if your business has the potential to become profitable—that is, if you take your time and do it correctly.

Create a spreadsheet that will list all of your income sources for the first year you will be in business.

Income

Income is the amount of money coming into your business. Consider all of your income sources, including sales from the DDC and any other services you might be offering. Project the dollar value of each income source in your spreadsheet across each month for the first year you'll be in business. These are not just figures for planning purposes—they will be your financial goal or target as each month goes by after you open.

Your income may come from the following:
- **Cash sales.** Once you know what you are able to charge for the DDC service in your area, you can estimate your monthly revenue and add it as a line item to your spreadsheet.
- **Boarding.** If you've decided to offer boarding services, estimate the revenue from this source. Your boarding service may take a few months to get off the ground, as clients may want to get to know you and your staff before leaving their dog overnight. Be conservative when estimating this income.
- **Grooming and training.** You may decide to offer additional services like grooming or

training. You can either hire someone as a permanent staff member to handle these services and estimate that income as a line item on your spreadsheet. Or you can hire a dog professional as an independent contractor —that way, you don't need to add the expense of another employee. With this type of arrangement, you'd come to an agreement about how to split the earnings (for example, 60/40). Your percentage should be entered as a line item.

- **A "pick-up and drop-off" service.** You may decide to add this type of service for a bit of extra income. While this can be a challenging service to pull off (especially when one of your employees is absent), it might just be the value-added service that some people need to get them to enroll. You can even subcontract this service out to a "doggy taxi service"—perhaps a pet sitter looking for additional income. Add this as a line item to the spreadsheet.
- **Retail.** Most doggy day care centers offer items to purchase in their reception area. They can run the gamut from shampoos and flea soaps to collars, leashes, pet food, toys, chews (like the ones Nylabone makes), and snacks. If you decide to add a retail outlet, keep in mind that you must file a quarterly sales tax report, accounting for all of the sales tax money collected for that three-month period. (Most of your DDC accounting software can track this for you—see Chapter 7 for more details.) If you plan to offer a retail store in your DDC, list the projected income from retail sales as a line item on your spreadsheet.

Expenses

Expenses are the amount of cash flowing out of your business—basically, the cost of doing business. Add the estimated expenses of running your DDC to your profit and loss statement. Project the dollar value of the expenses across each month.

- **Payroll.** List how much it will cost to pay your proposed staff as a line item on the spreadsheet.
- **Taxes.** Your town will be able to give you an idea of any taxes you'll have to pay. Seek the advice of a payroll professional to help you estimate your payroll taxes.
- **Insurance.** Contact an insurance agent and ask for an estimate.

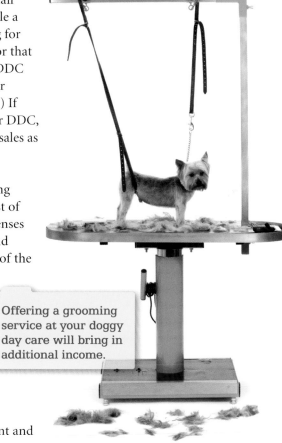

Offering a grooming service at your doggy day care will bring in additional income.

Insurance

When I opened my own business, there were not a lot of DDCs around, and the insurance company I contacted wasn't even sure what I needed. Luckily, this has changed, and your insurance agent will be able to guide you in deciding what you need because there are now standards for the business. Make sure that you are well covered—insurance is not the place to skimp! If you are renting a building, your landlord will probably require certain coverage.

- **Advertising.** Find out current rates for local newspaper ads, signage, radio, and perhaps even television ads. Decide what's reasonable for your budget, and plug the cost into your spreadsheet. (You'll tweak this number when you see how much actual revenue you are bringing in.)
- **Utilities.** If you are renting, your landlord should be able to provide average utility costs. If you have bought the building, the utility companies can give you a projection. It's important to find out these costs before signing the lease.
- **Loan Repayment.** The bank can give you a breakdown of monthly payments (i.e., loan amortization).
- **Equipment.** You should break your equipment purchases down into detail, and each one should be a line item.
- **Miscellaneous.** Add a line item for miscellaneous expenses and emergency contingencies. Depending on what you can afford, it is wise to add 10 to 25% of your total budget, broken down into 12 months, for unexpected events.

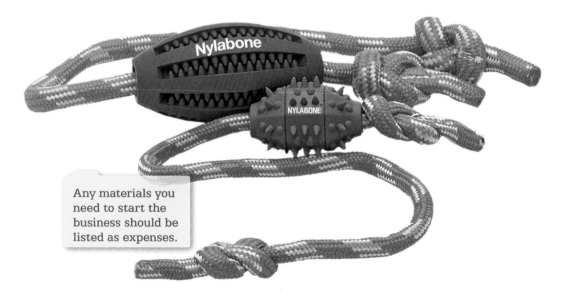

Any materials you need to start the business should be listed as expenses.

Final Touches

Finally, you'll want to make your business plan look professional by adding a table of contents. You'll also want to include any appendices, such as citations of town regulations, websites, sources of cost estimates, current tax rates, advertising quotes, etc.—items that aren't essential for the plan but are impressive to anyone reading it and deciding on lending capital. It also proves that you did your homework. You may also want to add any photos of the proposed facility and insert all of this material into an attractive folder or binder.

Because starting up a DDC is still relatively new and perhaps unfamiliar to some lending institutions, you will want to put your best paw forward. Take your time with the finishing touches on your business plan. Make your package reflect all of the study and research you have done.

You now have the core of your business plan and know exactly how much money you will need to start up your DDC and keep it going. You can now present this comprehensive business plan to financial institutions to ask for the loans required.

A Day in the Life

We had an adorable yellow Labrador Retriever at our day care who had the sweetest personality that you could ever imagine! She came in to board over the weekend, and we noticed throughout the day that she was having difficulty moving her bowels. We continued to watch her for possible signs of a blockage throughout the day. Later that day, she finally had a successful bowel movement. Oh, what a sight! Out came two pairs of brightly colored women's thongs. We were laughing as we picked them up (with latex gloves on) and put them into the washer.

When the owners came to pick up their dog, we also presented them with the laundered thongs. We told them the story, and they didn't seem surprised—apparently, their Lab eats a lot of things that shouldn't be eaten!

Lesson of the Day: Pay attention when dogs are trying to relieve themselves, and note what's in their stool. Any abnormality could be a sign of a bowel infection or digestive blockage, which can cause a dog to become critically ill. It is also wise to check with the owners to see if they suspect that the dog has ingested any material that could be harmful.

Chapter

4

Financing Your Doggy Day Care Center

Now that you're fully armed with a well-thought-out, comprehensive business plan, you're ready to try to find suitable funding.

Thisis easily the most pivotal time for you and your dog care business. If you can't get the required funding, you'll have to return to your routine job, save up more money, and go back to the drawing board. But if you do get the required funding, you'll be heading in a new and exciting direction.

Your Contribution

After working the financial numbers and plugging your best projections into your business plan, you now know how much money is required to start up and operate your DDC. Some of this start-up money must come from you as an individual. Financial lenders look unfavorably on supporting a prospective business owner who isn't contributing money to the enterprise. If you approach a lender with nothing to contribute to this significant investment, it shows little preparation on your part. It also indicates that you haven't been seriously planning for this major change and implies that you are not willing to take any real, personal financial risk at all.

Delaying Your Salary

Before you fully commit to this endeavor, you should have a small financial reserve to cover your personal expenses for up to six months (and some consultants even suggest a full year). If this is possible, you won't have to take any money out of the business for your own use. You can pay your employees and keep the business rolling along. Then after several months, when enrollment approaches capacity and cash flow is steady and growing, you can withdraw your salary or dividends from the business revenue. This is something that many new entrepreneurs overlook—they begin to take out profits immediately and have problems paying for things down the road.

Capital Investment

According to the American Kennel Association, 50% of all doggy day care centers start with less than $50,000 in capital investment, while about 25% start up with less than $25,000, leaving 25% that required more than $50,000.

Personal Sacrifice

To succeed in the first year of business, be prepared to tighten your belt. During this time, you must live leanly and only buy necessities. There will be no extravagances, expensive dinners, clothing, or vacations until your doggy day care business is stable and profitable. And don't fall into the trap of using credit cards to buy things—necessities or not. It's too easy to sink deeper into debt this way. If you have the passion for the business, then this personal sacrifice will come easily.

About Funding

Before you look for funding for your start-up business, there's a few things you need to know about loans.

Understanding Your Liability

Understanding your liability is crucial in the financial funding process. Many prospective business owners think that a business loan is forgiven if the business fails and the owner declares bankruptcy. This is not true.

When you apply for a loan, the lender will require some form of collateral insurance, which means that you must put up something equal in value to the face value of the loan. This is usually property, such as your house or other land you might own. Sometimes vehicles, boats, or other such items may be added to your collateral line, but they must come close to the current value of your loan.

If you default in repaying your loan, the lender takes ownership of the collateralized property, thereby ensuring that they are repaid one way or another. This concept is fair and common business practice. It also gives the prospective owner a significant incentive to do everything possible to make the business succeed.

Interest Rates

Now that you know the loan must be repaid regardless of the success or failure of your DDC, you should also understand that these loans can carry a significant interest rate. It can be 2 to 4 percent higher than conventional mortgage loans, so you're going to be paying back a painfully high amount of money for quite some time, depending on the amount you need and the rapidity of your business's growth.

Financing Your Doggy Day Care Center

The failure of a pet care business impacts the community, the owners, and the dogs.

The good news is that these institutions don't want you to fail. If you're struggling early on, they'd prefer that you come directly to them and let them know. This way, a solution can be arranged to prevent a painful situation later.

The Impact of Failure

Most of the time when a small business closes, the direct impact is only felt by the business owner. The "out of business" sign hung in the window may be a sad situation for the owner, but the community as a whole is relatively unaffected. But when it comes to care facilities like doggy day care centers, there will be many people in the community negatively impacted by the business failing and closing down. Not only will the business owner be affected, but the dogs and their owners will be impacted as well. They enrolled in your program, got used to the new lifestyle and routines with their new friends, and then business failure brought it all to an abrupt emotional end. For this reason, many lenders are especially sensitive about ensuring that a care-related business will succeed in their community.

Where to Look for Funding

There are many institutions in the business of lending money. Hopefully, you've gotten in touch with a SCORE counselor as I suggested in Chapter 3. Your counselor can provide you with detailed information about lenders in your community and give you the current record of those institutions lending money to small businesses (less than 500 employees). This information will include names of the recipients, how much money they were loaned, and which loan program was used.

Your SCORE counselor may also know which lenders would be more open to the concept of a doggy day care center, which might give you an edge on your application for funding. Certain institutions favor certain types of businesses, and I'm sure that there will be several lenders who favor animal care and associated service providers.

Local Banks

Local banks are very sensitive about providing small business loans and will most likely listen to your plan with intent. This is especially true if the center will be in the community and you will be providing jobs to local residents. Go online to check out your local bank's lending information. Some banks may have the necessary forms online, but some will require you to come in person.

Small Business Association Programs

The U.S. Small Business Administration (SBA) has a series of lending programs for small business loans that may be suitable for your day care center. It won't loan you the money directly but can guarantee loans through its lending partners. The loans depend on your potential and projected revenue for the business. Also, your location may dictate a preferred type of loan, depending on the lenders' program qualifications.

State Economic Development Organizations

Check out the economic development organization within your state or county, which assists in the start-up of small businesses. This information is readily available online—simply do a search for your state and the words "economic development." You'll be able to shop around for funding sources, and your SCORE counselor can help guide you through the pros and cons of each program.

Women in Business

There are a multitude of loans and grants available specifically for women entrepreneurs. Just search "women business loans" on the Internet and you'll find plenty of options.

Venture Capitalists

If more conventional loan channels won't work for you, venture capitalists are a source of funding you may want to consider. Typically, venture capitalists are a group of investors that capitalized your start-up operation, hoping for a quick turnaround on their investment. This type of lender might lend more readily than a bank and can provide capital resources quickly, which can get you up and running sooner than you thought. The downside is that they may want shares in your business as well as financial payments as part of the arrangement, so in effect you will not own your business. You'll be working for and reporting to others who often know nothing about your business. Plus, venture capitalists usually want the loan paid back much sooner than conventional lenders will.

Friends and Family

There is one other source of funding that many entrepreneurs turn to—borrowing from friends or family. I advise you to avoid this if at all possible. Often your loyal friends and relatives will want to see you live your dream of working with dogs and owning your own business. They may offer you some of their hard-earned savings to help you get started. While I know that every case is different, I strongly suggest using this financial resource only as a last resort. Many personal relationships suffer when things don't go quite right, resulting in resentment and anger. A small business loan is never worth the dissolution of a close relationship.

Business Plan Presentation

Once you've applied for small business funding, you will have to present your business plan to the lending institution. Ask in advance how many people will be in the meeting, and make sure that you have enough plans for everyone. Your business plan should be crisp and neat and presented in a nice folder. You can even add "Business Plan presented for [individual's name]" to the outside of the folder as a personal touch.

For your presentation, dress in business attire. The lenders will be looking at you as a direct reflection of the business. The way in which you present yourself will be a factor in their decision.

Practice your pitch with someone beforehand. This is a great way to ensure that you are expressing yourself with confidence and that you know your material inside and out. This is the time to show your enthusiasm and sell yourself.

The lender will be asking you questions, so be ready for them. Here are some of the things you may be asked:

- What is your competition?
- How are you going to repay the loan?
- What is the future of the industry?
- Have you ever been in business before?
- What are you bringing to the table (experience, money)?
- How are you going to bring business in?

Granted, most of this information will be covered in your business plan, but the lenders will want assurance you know your stuff! Because doggy day care is relatively new, they will be especially inquisitive about the business and your ability to operate it successfully. They will likely want to conduct a site visit to your intended location/facility.

After the meeting, send handwritten thank-you notes to each individual to express your appreciation for their time.

These presentations shouldn't be too stressful on you. Keep in mind that the lenders really do want to loan you the money. They just want to ensure that it is a good investment for them and for you!

Dress professionally for your business plan presentation.

See Your Accountant

When you succeed in getting your small business loan, the first person you should contact is your accountant. Sit down with her and discuss how to prudently use the money to start up your DDC. Ask how you should distribute your payments so that the balance can make money (interest) while it is not being used.

Keep in mind that your loan repayment is both an expense and a revenue adjuster. That is, the payments you make are expenses to your business and are reflected in your profit and loss statement from your accountant. The interest paid on your loan is also a deduction and reduces your tax liability. It's a good idea to understand the basics of these accounting issues, but leave it to the expert to work them out for you.

After you open your DDC, you should meet with your accountant at least once per quarter through the first year. Thereafter, you should only need to meet once or twice a year. Be prepared to discuss financial issues, expansion plans, unforeseen expenses, etc. Your accountant should have experience enough to advise you on all of these financial issues. You are paying for this service, so use it!

Dealing with the financing of your DDC can overwhelm you if you let it. Take things one step at a time, and remember that it's the little steps that will get you to your goal and help you realize your dream. The money is out there if you are persistent and willing to do the footwork.

A Day in the Life

For me, obtaining the loan to start up my DDC was one of the most challenging hurdles. My day care was the first one to be opened in my town, so many lenders didn't have faith that it would work or thought that it was too much of a gamble. Whether it was talking to the bank or people from the town, I received the same message—it wasn't possible. However, I knew that it would work and didn't have any hesitation at all. When I sat down with my SBA representative and told her I was mortgaging my house for some of the start-up money, she saw my determination and helped me convince others that I would make the business a success. My faith in myself and my plan eventually got me all the start-up funding I needed. That is the kind of determination lenders want to see.

Lesson of the Day: Do you have enough faith in yourself to put everything on the line? If you do, your lenders are sure to follow

Chapter

5

Design and Setup of Your Doggy Day Care Center

Now that your funding has been approved, you must carefully and thoughtfully design your doggy day care center.

You should have already created a very general design during the feasibility study, when you selected your building and prior to signing a lease. Now it's time to nail down the layout and image of how the center will look.

This is another instance where advice from a consultant or another DDC owner is useful. Your initial site visit(s) during the feasibility study should have provided you with a good idea of what's required, and someone with experience running a DDC can warn you about any pitfalls you may encounter with the "building out" of the facility.

General Requirements

Understand the goals of your business's physical layout before you get started. The right layout will give you a smooth-running, easily managed DDC. You must consider convenience in terms of the dogs' needs, the dog owners' needs, and of course, your staff members' needs.

The areas of the layout you need to consider are:

- bathroom (disabled accessible)
- kitchen/feeding area
- laundry room
- boarding area (optional)
- office
- day care area(s)
- outside area
- employee lounge
- play area
- grooming area (optional)
- reception/retail area
- hallways
- storage

Start this critical process by preparing draft drawings of these areas. There's usually no need to go to the expense of hiring an architect; several inexpensive computer software packages can help with this task. Or if you can draw freehand, now is the time to use your talents. Every detail for the areas should be laid out in your drawings.

Get permission from your landlord for your DDC build out, and show her the plans. You will also likely need to show the proposed layout to the town for approval. They will be looking for fire exits, disabled accessibility, and overall safety of the area. If you are taking over a building that already held a business, all of these things should be in order. It gets more complicated if you are refitting a warehouse or other space from scratch.

Let's take a closer look at each of these vital areas and what's included in the design and setup for each one.

Lease Tip

NEVER sign a lease without a contingency upon approvals from the town and the lending institution before the lease takes effect. You want to make sure that the zoning is correct so that you can obtain whatever permits and licenses are necessary (which will vary in each town). If you sign the lease without a contingency and the town determines that the zoning is wrong, you are on the hook for the lease.

Bathroom
Size
The size of the bathroom(s) will depend on your specific building layout.

Design and Setup
Your bathroom must be disabled accessible. You can get the specific requirements from your town, which may include wheelchair accessibility, installing grab bars, and preventing slippery flooring. In my DDC, I was required to install a strobe light outside of the bathroom in case of fire for anyone who could not hear the alarm.

Boarding Area (Optional)
If you are going to offer boarding services, this will be one of your easiest rooms to set up.

Size
This area will vary in square footage (sq m) depending on how many dogs you plan to board and the number and size of crates required.

Design
The room should be as comfortable for the dogs as possible, so make sure that you have sufficient heating in this room, as well as a couple of night-lights for the dogs. I also found it a nice touch to have soothing music playing in the background to help the pooches get to sleep. If you have the available space, think about offering private rooms for the dogs at a higher price.

If you are going to offer boarding at your DDC, you'll need crates of several different sizes.

Setup
You'll need a sufficient number and variety of crate sizes to fit all sizes of dogs. I've found plastic crates, like the ones Nylabone makes, easy to clean. You can easily drag them outside and spray them off versus trying to wipe down and dry metal crates. Whatever crates you choose, make sure that they are difficult to escape. The crates should not be placed too closely together to prevent any cage fighting.

Day Care Area
This is where the dogs will spend most of their day, either playing or sleeping.

Size
You should have between 70 to 100 square feet (21 to 30.5 sq m) per dog. If your business plan was developed anticipating growth to 50 dogs, the math is simple. You should have

roughly 3,500 to 5,000 square feet (1067 to 1524 sq m) for this focal area of your doggy day care center.

Although you want adequate space allocated for the doggy play area, the indoor space shouldn't be so large that the pooches will run around at top speeds. This is an important point that most DDC owners don't think about. Dogs will inevitably crash into the walls during play, but it's safer if they can't do this at top speed.

Design

The actual day care area may be one large room or several rooms dedicated to this purpose. If the area is one large space, you will need to use fencing to create separate areas. (See "Movable Fencing," below.)

Various types of flooring can serve the doggy play area quite well. Keep in mind that it will need to be mopped often and will take abuse. Depending on your budget, tile, cement, or rubber flooring is a good choice. I had the cement floor in my DDC painted with colored sand epoxy paint. It not only made the room brighter, but the infused sand made the floor skid-free. And the floor stood up to daily abuse and multiple mop cleanings.

Double doors or gates are important features. Chances are each time a door opens, one of the dogs will try to make his escape. You should install double doors that, when secured, will not be able to open very far. Make sure that the latches close easily on these doors—if they don't close by themselves, it's too easy for a dog to jump up on the gate and accidentally let all of the other dogs out! Gates and doors that automatically latch as soon as they're closed are also available.

Setup

Movable Fencing

As we discussed earlier, you must separate the dogs—not by breed but by size and temperament. Unless you have separated rooms, you'll need movable fences to partition off the large area.

The fencing must be tall enough to deter any dogs from trying to escape. The movable fence should be durable and about 5 to 6 feet (1.5 to 1.8 m) tall. The fences need to be movable in order to quickly change the configuration of the play area and other stations. Plus, you and the staff always need to be able to see the dogs. Minimally, the top half of the fencing should be see-through, like lattice or chain link. Plastic lattice works well because it's easy to clean and very durable. Wood is heavy, making it harder to move, and it's easily chewed.

Time-Out Crates

Provide a couple of time-out crates within each room or section for dogs who need to be given a break and can't calm down. It is not simply for punishment but provides them a few minutes alone to relax. Most dogs like to take a break and welcome the crates.

Stations

Stations are just designated areas where there are places to hang the poop baggies out of the dogs' reach. If you like, you could install shelving for this purpose, but just make sure that it's high enough that the dogs can't get at it.

Each station must have a sturdy bag of some sort in each corner to hold plastic baggies for picking up excrement. The poop bucket that the baggies are placed in should be kept outside of the day care area. Usually, it can be stored in the hallway area with an airtight lid.

Always keep spray bottles located within each station. These spray bottles are vital to breaking up rough play, mounting, or fighting. Please note: The spray bottles are *not* used for punishment. They are used as a determent to prevent escalating behavior with the dogs. You could also use noisemakers, such as a can filled with pennies, to distract the dogs.

A sharp pair of scissors should be kept hanging somewhere handy (but out of reach of the dogs) in case a dog gets caught in another dog's collar. This will happen when dogs are playful with one another or if they become aggressive and begin a fight.

Place a few hooks on the wall to hang leashes. You will use these often to take the dogs in and out of the day care with ease.

Water Stations

You will need several water stations placed around the play area. I prefer metal buckets because they are easy to clean. The water should be changed frequently and always kept clean. You might try raising the water stations on a small step stool against the wall, which I found deters dogs from jumping in to go for a swim!

Separate larger dogs from smaller dogs using moveable fencing.

Employees' Lounge

Designate an area for an employees' lounge.

Size and Design

The size and design will depend on your individual building.

Setup

The employee area should have a table and a few comfortable chairs. This can also serve as a place to sleep at night if you or one of your staff is staying over with boarding dogs.

Designate a separate area for feeding the dogs.

Feeding Area

Most DDCs don't routinely feed the dogs each day unless requested by the owner. Owners usually feed their pooch early in the morning and then again after picking him up. It's a good routine all the way around—what better way for the owner and dog to celebrate their reunion than with food! But for those dogs who need to be fed lunch, like puppies and boarding dogs, you'll need an area separate from the play area.

Size

The feeding area doesn't have to be large because you are not going to be feeding the dogs together anyway. In my DDC, this area was fairly large because I had a combination kitchen/grooming/laundry area. It really depends on your building and how creative you can get in your layout.

Design

You will want a separate area from the play area to feed the dogs. In my facility, it was easy to use the grooming area because that was empty for most of the day.

Setup

The feeding area should always have these items easily accessible:

- cabinets, cubbies, and plastic tubs to store the dog food
- cleaning products
- disposable paper feeding trays or metal bowls
- masking tape to label individual dog's food
- microwave oven
- sink
- small refrigerator
- utensils
- water bowls
- white board to track the feeding schedule

It's important to be organized, or you will run into problems such as forgetting to feed a dog, feeding a dog twice, or feeding him another dog's food. You'll end up dealing with diarrhea from a dog with an upset stomach, followed by informing the dog owner about your error.

Grooming Area (Optional)

You will need an area dedicated to grooming if you are planning to offer this service.

Size

You must have enough room for a tub and a grooming table, plus some room to move around. The size will vary depending on how many grooming tables you install.

Design

If you are qualified and plan to do your own grooming, you can design the layout yourself. (Check to see if you have the proper credentials to perform this service in your state or county.) If, however, you plan to subcontract out to a groomer who will come to your DDC, you may want to include her during this process. After all, she is the expert and can come up with the best working layout.

The key to laying out the grooming area is to have quick access to everything you need. Some dogs don't like being bathed and brushed, so the sooner it's over, the better. Design the space so that everything is quickly within reach.

Setup

Bathing Area

Your grooming area will need to have a good-sized tub (preferably elevated to prevent too much bending). For dogs who are too heavy to lift into the tub, have some sort of ramp so that they can walk up into the tub. Make sure that you have a hook attached to the wall to attach a leash so that the dogs will not be able to jump out. Use a nonslip mat in the

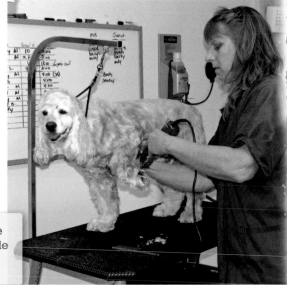

A grooming table with an adjustable arm keeps dogs safe.

bottom of the tub, which will keep the dogs from slipping.

Next to the tub, place plastic drawers and/or cabinets that will hold all of the cleaning products. You will also need easy access to drying towels.

Bathing and Care Supplies

The following supplies should be located near the tub. Rolling plastic drawers or shelves above and within reach of the tub are good options. You should minimally have the following list of items:

- brushes
- canine toothpaste
- combs
- conditioner
- cotton balls
- cotton swabs
- ear cleaner
- eye cleaner
- leashes
- muzzles
- nail clippers
- petroleum jelly
- shampoos (all types—medicated and regular)
- styptic pen or powder
- tick tweezers
- toothbrushes
- towels

Grooming Supplies

You will need a grooming table with an adjustable arm to secure the dog for the drying and clipping process. For dogs who are too large for the grooming table, place a hook on the wall to hold them during the drying process.

You should also have easy access to the following supplies:

- bandanas
- brushes
- clipper blades
- clipper cleaners
- clippers
- colognes
- combs
- dematting tools
- dryers (handheld dryer, hair dryer, and cage dryer)
- leashes
- shedding blade
- strippers

Hallways

Although you are going to need to store things in your hallway, it shouldn't be cluttered. Hallways must always be clear enough for staff to walk through quickly in case of emergencies.

Design and Setup

Areas of your hallway can be used to hold your mop buckets and hoses (to fill water and mop buckets and clean floors). Most of these items can be hung from the walls of the hallway, which provides easy access but won't create clutter. I found it useful to put some sort of matting underneath the mop buckets and water stations to catch any spillage. You will also want to leave your poop buckets (with a secured lid) in the hallway so that dogs can't get into them.

Laundry Room

You will need a laundry room in your DDC. You'll be surprised how quickly your laundry adds up from towels, bedding, and cleaning rags.

Size

Your laundry room should have enough room for a washer and dryer and folding area. Probably a couple hundred square feet (sq m) will suffice. This area could be combined with another room.

Design

If you have a grooming area, it's convenient to locate it there because this makes washing up all of the bath towels much easier. It's a good idea to have a sink available in this area as well for washing hands and other cleaning needs.

Setup

You'll need a heavy-duty, commercial-type washing machine so that it doesn't break down from overuse. This room will also require a clothes dryer with proper ventilation. The filters must be checked nightly and kept clean. They fill up quickly, not only from towel lint but from the dog hair that flies around the space.

Areas of your hallway can be used to hold hoses for easy clean up.

Office

You must be organized in the office area. When 30 to 50 dogs are coming to your center every day, it's easy to get behind in your paperwork.

Size

Generally, an area with about 70 to 80 square feet (21 to 24 sq m) will be adequate for the office, but if you have the space, try to make it as large as possible. You will use it for interviewing dog owners and applicants and to hold staff meetings.

Design

Design this space yourself at the beginning of the process and not as an afterthought. You want the office to be conducive to detailed work and to serve as a refuge from the energetic, noisy dog play area. So don't gloss over the design quickly.

The office should be segregated from the play areas so that you can concentrate on administrative tasks. You might consider soundproof insulation installed in your office walls. There should be a glass window with blinds or shades so that you can observe the play area at your discretion

Keep your office area organized.

Setup

Organization

You will need at least one large filing cabinet for all of your clients' folders and for various office supplies.

Computer Hardware

You should have a computer system that includes a printer (preferably a printer, scanner, fax combination). I found it helpful to acquire an "e-fax," which enables fax messages to come directly to your computer via e-mail instead of paying for a separate fax line. When picking your computer hardware, it should be high quality because you want it to last three years or more. Also, make sure that you have a computer technical service nearby or have a maintenance contract with the computer manufacturer.

Business Software

I highly recommend that you purchase business software created specifically for running a dog care business. A variety of these products are available with a range of applications that will make your administrative tasks much easier. Take care to select software that works for you. More information about business software is discussed in Chapter 7.

Outside Area

The outside area is an extension of the indoor dog play area. It should always be kept clean and inviting for the dogs to come out from time to time (weather permitting) to enjoy a change of scenery and take in whiffs of clean air.

Size

The size of the enclosed outdoor area will depend on the building and property you end up in and the amount of dogs in your day care. I had a 3,000-square-foot (914-sq-m) day care, and my outside area was 1,000 square feet (305 sq m). This is just a general idea—it can be bigger or smaller, and you'll just have to adjust the number of dogs let out at one time.

Design

First and foremost, the outside area needs to be safely enclosed. Fencing should be at least 6 feet (2 m) tall, solid, and sealed off to the public. With fewer distractions from the outside, the dogs will be quieter, and it will also prevent someone from sticking a hand through the fence and getting bitten. Have a gate that leads to the outside of the fenced area—but *only* for emergencies. At all other times, this gate should be locked to prevent escapes.

There are many types of ground cover available for the outside area, including grass, cement, rocks, and mulch. What I've found works best is a poured cement deck. We had it sloped toward the outside perimeter that led into a moat just outside of the fence. When we washed the outside deck down, the soiled water ran off the deck and into the moat. The one downside of cement decking is that it heats up quickly, but you can provide some artificial shade to prevent this.

No matter what type of ground cover you choose, the outside area has to be washed down nightly to prevent diseases from spreading and odors from occurring.

Putting up some sort of an awning outside will allow you to deal with different types of weather. It will keep the dogs dry during rain or snow and provide shade from the hot summer sun.

Setup

The outside area should have a water hose handy to clean the grounds and to serve as a deterrent for dog fighting. Buckets of water should also be available to the dogs for drinking. As suggested earlier, putting the buckets up on a step stool will help keep the dogs from showing off their best swimming strokes.

You will also need a tightly sealed poop bucket for the outside area. And if you have the room, you can provide a kiddie swimming pool for the dogs to jump in and take a swim.

Reception/Retail Area

The design of the retail/reception area is important because it's the first area your clients will see upon arrival. It is your welcome area for dogs and dog owners alike. You always want to make sure that this room is kept clean and presentable, with attractive accoutrements!

Size

Generally, your DDC reception and retail area requires about 160 square feet (49 sq m).

Design

Make this room warm and welcoming to the owners and dogs. You should have a checkout counter where clients will be greeted and where customers can pay their bills. Place a computer at the front desk to check in dogs and make reservations. You'll also need a phone in this area. I suggest getting a main base phone with multiple cordless units so that wherever you are, you'll be able to answer the phone. A cash register is nice but not a necessity—you can always use a cashbox instead. A credit card machine should also be at the desk.

This is also the area where you'll display your dog items for sale, so it should always be well organized. Have shelves for flat items and display racks for leashes, collars, toys, doggy treats, etc.

Setup

It's a good idea to set out some chairs so that the reception area can serve as a small waiting space for those coming in for an interview.

Make sure your reception area is welcoming.

If you're going to have "cubbies" to store the dogs' belongings, they should be flush against one of the walls of the reception area. These should be neat and clearly labeled with the dogs' names.

Although this area is used for many basic functions, think about adding some personality and life to it as well. During the month, I would take 20 to 30 photos of the dogs at play and post them on one of the walls in the reception area. Owners would come in each day and immediately go to the photos on the wall. They'd look for their pooch and get a kick out of seeing their dog having fun. I also had a large framed photo for "Dog of the Month." This wasn't a contest per se, as every dog had a turn at the honor, but the clients loved it.

Another personal touch I found useful was hanging a small bulletin board in the reception area. I would post local "doggy news" (any material I came across that might interest my clients), and I allowed my clients to use this bulletin board for anything appropriate but not necessarily related to dogs. They would post flyers for garage sales or other items for sale such as cars, houses, or boats. My clients appreciated this "Wall of Fame" (and I like to think the dogs did too!).

You can have a "Dog of the Month" feature in your reception area.

DOG OF THE MONTH

NOaH

Hi there, my name is Noah! I have grown up in doggy day care since I was 12 weeks old. I couldn't play with the other dogs there until I had all of my shots, but as soon as I did, I was right in there with all of my new friends. I'm three years old now and have a face only a mother could love...well, that's not totally true. Everybody loves me!!!

What I like most about coming to day care is playing with all of the friends I have made. I'm never bored, and I get a lot of exercise and attention. There is always something going on! I can run around or take a nap. It doesn't matter to me as long as I'm with my friends!

Congratulations to Our Very Special Dog of the Month!

Four Legs Good
Where Your Dog Is Always In Good Hands

Storage

Your storage area needs to be clean and neat at all times. It's the only way to prevent pest infestation.

Size

This area should be large enough to store all of the necessary items to run your DDC. Depending on your supplies and inventory, plan on about 80 square feet (24 sq m) for storage.

Design

This room can become disorganized quickly. I recommend using a system with labeled plastic tubs so that you can find things quickly when you need them.

Setup

The storage area is where you'll leave your vacuums, cleaning buckets, and other tools for easy access. You'll need sturdy shelving, which comes in handy to store dog food, paper products, cleaning supplies, etc. If you sell the large bags of commercial dog food to your customers, you need to have heavy-duty steel racks to hold them. Keep an inventory of your retail items in the storage area.

Start-Up Inventory List

To make your setup a bit easier, I've created a list of the basic items you'll need to start up your DDC.

Day Care Equipment and Supplies

- bleach
- broom and dustpan
- cleaning buckets
- detergent
- dog food
- first-aid kit (see Appendix B)
- floor vacuum
- garbage bags, regular and extra heavy duty
- garbage cans
- glass cleaner
- kennel cleaner
- masking tape
- mop buckets
- mops
- paper food trays for feeding
- paper towels
- plastic gloves
- poop buckets

> Keep your cleaning supplies handy but out of reach of the dogs.

- rags
- scrub brushes
- small baggies (flap top)
- small refrigerator
- sponges
- toolbox
- washer and dryer
- water buckets for each room and outside
- wet/dry erase board
- wet vacuum

Grooming Supplies
- bandanas with your logo (optional)
- blade cleaner
- brushes
- clipper blades
- clippers
- conditioner
- cotton balls
- cotton swabs
- doggy cologne
- dryers, hand and cage
- ear cleaner
- eye wipes
- finger brushes
- flea combs
- grooming table with adjustable arm
- muzzles
- nail clippers
- nail grinder
- rakes
- ramp
- scissors
- shampoo, medicated and regular
- shavers
- shedding blades
- slip leashes
- styptic power or pen
- towels
- tub

Design and Setup of Your Doggy Day Care Center

Boarding Supplies

- bedding
- crates—small, medium, and large sizes
- large plastic bags (to cover beds)
- packing blankets

Office Supplies

- brochures
- business cards
- clipboards
- computer system
- desk
- filing cabinets
- folders
- highlighters
- intake forms
- masking tape
- paper
- pens (with your logo)
- phone system
- staplers
- walkie-talkies
- wet/dry bulletin board and markers
- wireless webcam (optional)

A tall, solid fence is perfect to enclose the outside area and keep everyone safe.

Retail Products (General Categories)

- chews
- clothing (with your logo)
- collars
- flea and tick prevention
- food
- grooming products
- leashes
- toys
- treats

Take time to design your day care. Think about the functionality of the space—you want it to flow. For example, you don't want your entrance gate around the other side of the building—it should be next to the lobby for easy access. Think about your everyday activities and how you can make the operations easy and effective.

A Day in the Life

As the first doggy day care to open on Cape Cod, Massachusetts, we were sailing into uncharted waters. It seemed that everything we did was by trial and error. Although we had planned thoroughly, we still felt that we started the business by the seat of our pants!

We had shelving built that ran all along the top of the daycare room, which we used to store our stock of paper towels—easy access to clean up messes.

One day the phone rang in the office, and I left the day care room for just a few minutes to answer it. Because the business had just begun and the dog census was low, I was the only one working that day. Upon my return to the play area, it looked as if a blizzard had hit the day care. All of the paper towel rolls were shredded into the smallest pieces possible. The dogs were looking at me like they knew they had done something wrong, but I couldn't get mad at them for two reasons. First, they looked so funny with little pieces of paper towel hanging off their fur, coming out of their mouths, and all over the floor! Second, I'm the one who left the paper towels in plain view and left the dogs alone to take the phone call.

Lesson of the Day: Give a lot of thought to the design of your DDC—anything left out that the dogs can access will end up causing problems!

Chapter

6

Staffing Your
Doggy Day Care Center

While the build out and design of your facility
is taking place, you can spend time selecting
and hiring your dog care staff.

There's an old saying about staffing: Hire slow and fire fast! Unfortunately, most people do just the opposite. Many business owners are ill prepared to thoroughly interview prospective employees—the people who will have enormous impact on the success of your DDC. After all, you are asking the clients who enroll their dogs at your center not only to trust you but your staff as well. These dogs are important members of their family, and your clients need to feel assured that the humans who will be looking after their dogs all day, every day, are responsible, sensitive providers.

How Many Employees Do I Need?

The rule of thumb is one staff member for every seven dogs. This is the ideal ratio and can vary a bit, depending on your mix of large and small dogs. If you have primarily large dogs, the 1 to 7 ratio is mandatory; but if you find that you have more small pooches, you might extend that ratio. Because the mix can change easily, it is wise to be one person overstaffed.

Finding Employees

The one mistake I made looking for employees was to advertise for two positions in the local newspaper. Within a few days, I had more than 75 calls, letters, and e-mails—it was overwhelming to say the least! Plus, most of the people who answered the ad were unqualified. They had no idea what it would be like to care for 30 to 50 dogs simultaneously, and they had no concept of all the dirty tasks that would be required. You'll get the same kind of response with posting on an Internet job site—you'll get a lot—and I mean a lot—of responses that you'll need to filter.

Try a Focused Approach

Before placing an ad in the local newspaper or on the Internet, consider a more focused approach for looking for qualified help. Contact local veterinary clinics, pet supply stores, grooming shops, and kennels—these businesses will usually allow you to post a flyer or ad on their public bulletin boards. Often they will immediately know of people who would be interested in your program.

Another venue to explore is local dog shows or other events that feature dogs. You can leave colorful flyers or your business card on vehicle windshields parked near these events.

Politeness Pays

Even if someone unqualified applies for a job at your DDC, it is important to respond with some type of formal answer. Everyone who comes in contact with your business should have a positive experience—they (or their friends) may become future customers! In my case, when I had 75 unqualified applicants from a newspaper ad, I called each and every one and cordially listened to why they wanted the job. Some of the people I turned down remembered me and my business and later enrolled their dogs in my DDC.

I have found that the best workers are those who plan to have a future career working with animals, such as veterinary technician students, or those who have a great deal of compassion and have worked at humane societies or other voluntary animal care organizations. So try posting flyers at schools with vet tech programs or your local SPCA.

The point is not to cast too wide of a net so that you can locate the right people. You need to be selective and reach the people who have experience with dogs or perhaps have worked with many dogs at one time.

Posting "help wanted" ads on the Internet might cast too wide a net—try a more localized approach first.

The Screening Process

Once you have enough queries, a courtesy phone call can help you screen out ineligible applicants. The following questions will help determine if a candidate can move on to the interview process. During your brief (approximately five-minute) phone conversation, ask the following:

- What hours are you available to work?
- Can you work weekends, early evenings, and holidays?
- Do you have any physical limitations, including allergies?
- Do you have any experience in multi-dog settings, including experience with large dogs?
- Do you understand the less desirable aspects of the business, including washing up excrement and vomit, constant cleaning, and handling overexcited dogs?
- Have you ever worked with the general public in a previous job? (Ask for details.)
- Why do you want to work at a dog day care center?

At the end of the call, tell the applicant that you will be calling back only if you feel that there is interest on your part. This way, you can avoid calling the applicant again to inform her you have selected someone else.

If you ask the questions above during the short phone call, you will screen out many unqualified people, leaving the remainder eligible for an interview. Prioritize the candidates who you think are the best qualified based on your phone screening, and schedule them first. Keep other potentials in a folder for future hirings. These people may be candidates for future positions through attrition or expansion.

The Interview Process

Before you interview the potential hire, ask her to fill out an application for employment. (A sample "Application for Employment" can be found in the Appendix: Form 3.) Once she has completed the application, it's time for the interview.

There is a simple rule to interviewing people: The applicant should talk 75% of the time and the interviewer 25% of the time. So if the interview takes about an hour, you should have spoken for 15 minutes and the applicant should have talked for 45 minutes. If you follow this rule, you will have a much better understanding of the person you are considering hiring.

You ideal candidate is not just a dog lover but someone who understands dogs.

The cardinal sin in an interview is when the hiring manager gets carried away describing her experience, philosophies, and values. At the end of the hour, the applicant leaves without the manager knowing anything about her experience, philosophies, and values.

If you feel uncomfortable or inexperienced interviewing potential hires, consider using a consultant to teach you how to effectively interview and hire staff. It's best to use a consultant familiar with the dog day care business who has hired this type of employee in the past.

Nondiscrimination

During an interview, you must strictly avoid any discriminatory questions. Nothing should be asked about the individual's personal life unrelated to the position being filled. This includes age, sexual orientation, club memberships, and almost any activity taking place outside of the workplace.

Questions to Ask

Your role in the interview is to ask the hard questions about the applicant's experience as it relates to the care of dogs, including:

- Have you ever worked with dogs before? In what capacity?
- Have you worked with multiple dogs?
- Are you comfortable around many energetic dogs?
- Are you confident that you can be in charge at all times and not the animal?
- Are you able to identify any illnesses in dogs?

- Have you ever had to break up dog fights? If so, how did you do it?
- How do you react in crisis situations? Can you give me an example?

Although there are some things you can't ask applicants, you can (and should) ask them about their work history even if it's not related to dog care. This can tell you a lot about a person. Questions to ask about job history include:

- Why did you take [particular job], and did you leave? (If they were let go, you can ask why they were fired.)
- What did you like about your prior jobs?
- How do you feel about your prior boss or supervisor?
- What didn't you like about your last position?
- What was your least favorite part of the job—paperwork, intersocial contact, other employees, punctuality, etc.?

Remember, this is your business. Who you hire is a reflection of your DDC. You are looking for someone who works independently and has basic common sense. The candidate should be a self-starter, love working with animals, and interact well with clients.

Managing Dogs

My doggy day care center manager told me he could sense those who would work out in the first five minutes of an interview. It comes down to the difference between someone who's simply a dog lover and someone who understands dogs. The latter is someone who controls or manages the dog and will always be in charge when the pooch demonstrates unacceptable behavior.

Information to Provide

You must provide the applicants with a detailed job description. Also explain that from time to time, there may be tasks that are not specific to the job description. The applicant must leave the interview understanding that you are not just hiring employees—you are assembling a *team*. You are looking for team members who will work together and get the job done—day after day!

If you find that there are several qualified candidates, ask some if they would consider filling in on an as-needed basis. This type of arrangement might appeal to them, and it will help you in times of staffing emergencies.

First-Aid Training

It's an excellent idea to have every one of your staff members learn pet first aid, including CPR. The Red Cross offers training classes specifically for the treatment of animals at many of their locations. Centers that offer these classes can be found at https://www.crossnet.org/services/hss/courses/pfachapter.html.

Trial Day

After the interview, if you are interested in a prospective employee, have her come in for a one-day observation. I've found it extremely helpful—the potential employee has no surprises about the environment or what the job entails, and you are able to see firsthand if this person can handle a pack of dogs. You might even consider creating "testing situations" during the trial day to observe how the candidate reacts to the dogs, the dog owners, and other staff.

It usually takes just a few hours for the applicant to decide that this is a job that appeals to her. And believe it or not, the reactions of the dogs to the potential employee are a great indicator of whether she is right for your facility. The dogs will show you if they are comfortable with the new person.

Most importantly, you can observe the reactions of the applicant to everything that goes on in your DDC and know rather quickly if this person will be good for the team.

Even if she does not work out, you'll still need to pay her for the trial day and list her as an "independent contractor" for your tax filings.

Training

The day care attendant job is not hard to learn, but your new hires will still be on a learning curve the first few weeks. It is imperative that your entire staff be on the same page, so make sure that any new hires are set up with a current, trusted employee and allowed to follow her around. A little bit of time spent on this type of training will make running your DDC easier.

Some employees will learn quicker then others, and some will be better at certain jobs than others. To get the most out of your employees, help them shine in whatever area they excel. You'll get more from your employees by encouraging them to grow than by criticizing them for their failings.

Employee Manual

Prepare a "policies and procedures manual" for your day care. It doesn't have to be extensive, but it should include the rules you want your employees to follow. It can consist of the following:

- your vision and purpose for your business, including your mission statement
- the responsibilities of employees, including job descriptions
- conditions of employment
- conditions for termination
- compensation

Experience handling multiple dogs is a plus in a potential hire.

- benefits
- safety in the workplace
- behavior that will not be tolerated (e.g., drinking, drugs, etc.)
- disciplinary procedures
- leave of absence

You may also want to establish a dress code and spell it out in your manual. Your staff should be required to wear shirts or sweatshirts with your logo. Some DDCs use scrubs as a viable alternative because they are easy to clean and monogram with your logo. I'd also recommend name tags, if possible. Even though it's a physical job, don't tolerate ripped clothing. Your staff members are a reflection of your business when they are working.

Hiring a person is easy, firing is difficult. The more you find out about potential staff members before you hire them, the easier it will be for you to manage your business after the candidate is on board. One last note on staffing—if you've hired an employee with a negative attitude, and you can't get her to change her ways, it's probably best that you part company. Negativity will just get the rest of your staff's morale down and will endanger the working environment of your DDC.

A Day in the Life

When I started my DDC, I didn't have much experience hiring people. I tended to base my decision on who I thought was "nice." One day a woman stopped in and seemed to have the one credential I thought was most important: She liked dogs. I hired her on the spot (bad idea!) and told her to be in the following morning at 6:00 a.m. She showed up sometime after 6:30 a.m. the next morning—not a good sign to be late on your first day. She was sluggish and tired but managed to look perfect in her expensive white pants and perfectly done nails. As she began to follow me around for her training lessons, we let the first dog out of his crate. Unfortunately, he didn't make it outside in time (this happens sometimes) and pooped on the floor. She stood there and watched and made no move to clean it up. So I asked her to grab a poop bag and some cleaning items and take care of it. She looked at me like I was crazy, then proceeded to ask me for a mask and some gloves because the mess was so distasteful to her. Let's just say that DDC employee turned out to be a very short-lived career move on her part!

Lesson of the Day: Hire slow and fire fast—I've said it before, but it's worth repeating! Working at a DDC is rewarding but certainly not glamorous. Only hire people who fully understand what the job entails.

Chapter

7

Operating Your
Doggy Day Care Center

Your facility is set up, your staff is hired, and you are finally ready to open your day care. So what can you expect running this unique business? This chapter will give you a taste of what the nature of the business is like.

We'll take a look at the five main players who compose your business: dogs, owners, staff, vendors, and community. These players are interdependent, and if managed properly, can help ensure a greater degree of success for your business. We'll also cover the aspects of the daily operations of your DDC.

Dogs

Although the dogs are not your customers per se, they are part of your clients' families and are precious to them. A happy dog will make for a happy client, so keeping the dogs content and safe will be your and your staff's top priority each day.

Before accepting any dog into your DDC, you must thoroughly evaluate him.

Evaluating the Dogs

Before you allow a dog into your day care, you'll have to evaluate him. Set up an evaluation session with a potential client, and ask her to bring her dog. When she arrives at your DDC, ask her to fill out an "Intake Application." (For a sample, see Appendix: Form 4.) One you have the client's basic information, you can move on to evaluating the dog to see if you will accept him.

Getting a feel of which dogs to accept will eventually become second nature to you, but in the beginning, it takes a bit of practice. Just one out-of-control dog can make your whole day a challenge.

First, ensure that the dog:
- is neutered or spayed if he is five to six months old and older
- is currently on a flea and tick prevention program
- has all of his necessary shots, with proof from the vet
- is in overall good health

If these basics are covered, you can move on to evaluating his personality. Spend some time with the dog, and take note of how he reacts to you and your staff.

- Is he easygoing?
- Does he growl?
- Does he have any problems being touched around the face and collar area?
- Is he aggressive or overly shy?
- Is he afraid of loud noises?
- Is he easily approachable?

This evaluation will help you weed out dogs who won't be able to adjust to day care. (Chapter 9 has more information about evaluating dogs.)

What's Day Care Like for the Dogs?

Most of the dogs who come to your day care facility will have had no previous experience in such an environment. They spent each day alone in a quiet, comfortable home. They have their favorite sleeping places and are comfortable with the layout of the house and the routine noises both inside and outside. They know where their water and food bowls are and where they left their favorite toys. But in this comfortable environment, there is no opportunity for socialization, and most dogs spend these lonely hours sleeping

Now picture this passive dog entering your DDC. Imagine the shock! It's a totally different world for him. There are barking noises that aren't coming from him but from other dogs; and these dogs are sharing a play area! Other dogs approach him as a pack, seeming to move in unison. Some are his size, and some are bigger or smaller. The scents he's detecting are different than those at home. There are many new things for him to explore and investigate.

Expect Different Reactions

The new dog, much like a small child, has to be treated sensitively for a few days until he becomes acclimated to your DDC. Fortunately, most dogs welcome the change and begin socializing immediately. They'll pick up the pack mentality and soon forget their lonely days of being left in their quiet, boring home. Typically, the newcomer will want to meet all of the other dogs, which requires a lot of walking and trotting around to interact with them. He'll be exhausted, especially after the initial introduction to the day care center, so be sure to explain this to his owner so that there's no surprise when all he wants to do when he gets home is rest. As the dog gets acclimated to the environment, he'll balance out his energy spurts, probably by taking short naps on the beds you've

New dogs may be cautious at first but will usually settle down nicely.

provided. This is the ideal balance for a dog at a DDC: socialization, exercise, and rest.

Some dogs may react a bit differently. They may become overstimulated when first introduced to so many new things and may vomit with excitement or bark like they've never barked before. Conversely, some dogs might react shyly, overloaded from the new experience. You'll have a staff member working with the dogs who will monitor the newcomer's reactions, help make him feel comfortable, and acclimate him to the new environment.

Unfortunately, there will be a few dogs who are unable to make the transition. Usually, these dogs (for whatever reason) are unable to socialize with 30 or 40 dogs at one time. It may be that they have been in their quiet home environment too long and can't handle the change. If little or no progress is seen in a dog's acclimation, he may not be a candidate for the day care center. It's not an easy topic to discuss with the client and must be handled sensitively.

Good communication with your clients is essential to keeping them happy.

Clients

Handling your clients will be an essential part of running your doggy day care.

Contracts

Before a client's dog steps foot in your DDC, she must sign your "Day Care & Boarding Requirements" form and a "Client Agreement" form. These forms will serve as the basis for the contract between you and the dog owner and spell out responsibilities and liability issues. (For samples, see Appendix: Form 5 and Form 6.) You should have a lawyer review these forms or help you develop your own to make sure that your business is legally covered in the event of a lawsuit.

Interacting With Clients

As we've already discussed, every owner thinks that her dog is the most precious in the world and is the only dog who matters. It's a syndrome particular to all day care centers, whether for pets or children. You and your staff must understand this and react accordingly—yet still stay professional.

The dog owner may come to you with a laundry list of specific likes or dislikes for her dog or demand special attention for him. It is up to you and your staff to let the owner know early that the dog will be treated well but will have the same attention and care as all of the other dogs. Barring any specific medical issue, he will blend in with the pack's routines. It is always best to be pleasantly direct with the dog owner and make her understand that the socialization the dog receives from interacting with the pack is the best thing for her beloved pooch.

Developing a Relationship

While you can't compromise the philosophy of your dog day care business by singling out one dog for special treatment, you can (and should) make the owner feel special. After all, the dog owner ultimately pays the bills. It's your client who will tell others about her experience with your center, and this word-of-mouth appraisal will ultimately recruit other dog owners to use your service. Extending common courtesy and politeness to every client will go a long way in building your business.

Start building a professional relationship with the dog owner as soon as possible. Take a few minutes each day to tell your client how her dog behaved that day. Emphasize the happiness the dog experienced while socializing and playing with the other dogs. Mention something specific about the dog's personality, and applaud his adaptation to the pack environment. By doing this, you'll reaffirm that the dog owner made the right decision enrolling in your day care center. You can even fill out a "Report Card" (see Appendix: Form 7) that lets your client know how her dog is doing. This can be done weekly or monthly.

From time to time, spend extra time with the owner to discuss what you think may be good for the dog in terms of new toys, more exercise, a change in diet, or scheduling grooming services. This reinforces that you have the owner's dog in mind and his best interests at heart. It's simple psychology but makes the owner feel that you truly care for her dog. As long as you are sincere, the owner will be happy to hear this information.

Unfortunately, not every conversation you have with your client will be positive. But you must be quick to tell the owner any negative news about her pooch. If the dog is antisocial, the owner should be informed immediately. If you decide that you must release the dog from enrollment, it shouldn't come as a surprise to his owner. You should have already warned her of the problems and suggested that the dog may be better off in

Business Strategies With Clients

If you have cultivated a good relationship with your clients, consider asking them to write a brief recommendation of your day care services. It always helps your business to have testimonials from people related to your day care center. If they agree, you could use these testimonials on your website, as well as in your marketing materials.

Another good business strategy is to let your clients do the marketing and recruiting for you. For anyone who brings in a new customer, you could offer a free week of day care or a night of boarding after a successful recruitment. Your business can increase quite a bit based on word-of-mouth referrals.

a different environment. This type of situation should be covered in the agreement signed by the dog owner.

Illness or Injury

One of the most difficult things to discuss with a client is a suspected illness or injury to the dog. In the case of an injury, you must be prepared to tell the owner the symptoms and probable cause. It's hard to do because the owner left the dog's safety in your hands, but ignoring it is not an option. You need to tell the owner everything, and above all, be honest. Your client will appreciate your openness and understand that you reacted to the problem in a professional way.

Injuries can include slight sprains, bruises, or sometimes serious dog bites. You and your staff should be trained to deal with minor injuries, but you'll need to know when to take the dog to a veterinarian in the case of a severe problem. Any injuries that happen at your DDC should be reported using an "Incident Report." (See Appendix: Form 8.) Give a copy to the owner, and keep a copy for your records.

It gets more difficult when you notice a potential medical problem. You may discover a mass on the dog's body or notice various other physical changes. In older dogs, this could indicate a serious situation, but you and your staff observing any such changes early could be the difference between a good prognosis and a dire one. Obviously, you must immediately let your client know what you've discovered so that she can take it from there.

If it's bad news, it will not only affect the emotions of your client but you and your staff as well. It's inevitable that you will have cultivated a special relationship with the dog, so the entire staff must be prepared for these situations.

During this somber period, be sensitive to the dog owner. Ask what you can do to help, and accommodate her wishes. Remember, the dog owner is your client but you usually end up as friends, and she'll need to be treated with respect and sensitivity at all times.

Good leadership skills are important for handling the dogs, as well as your staff.

Staff

As we mentioned in Chapter 6, hiring the best candidates for your staff is critical. These are the people who are on the front lines of your business each and every day. They will not only interface with the dogs but with your clients as well. Hopefully, you have found staff members who have a great work ethic and who are loyal to you and the dog day care business.

Leadership

Loyalty to an owner or manager needs to be earned. Spend time with your employees, be open to suggestions, and be a good leader to your staff. Probably the most important aspect of leadership is setting an example yourself for your staff to follow. This means that you must be a hands-on owner, not an absentee owner.

I was at my DDC almost every day. I would typically come in early in the morning and not leave until evening—seven days a week—until my business was running smoothly and my staff could be relied upon. But even then I wouldn't spend too much time away—I was still spending 50 to 60 hours per week there on a routine basis.

Something nice happens when employees see the boss doing the same tasks (including the dirty ones!) they have to do each day. It builds respect, enhances your leadership, and encourages loyalty.

Handling the Staff

Your staff members should always know how they are doing at their jobs. I always publicly thanked my employees in the presence of other staff and/or customers so that they knew I authentically felt they deserved the praise. And complimenting staff publicly gives them a boost of self-esteem that can further enhance their job performance.

You must also be prepared to reprimand an employee for poor job performance, sloppy work, or chronic tardiness or absenteeism. However, this is something that should be done in private with just you and the employee—and should be kept private. Confidentiality is a facet of good employer–staff relationships, and it too will be respected by your employees and earn you loyalty.

Staff Meetings

Your staff will be closest to the dogs, physically and emotionally, so they will know more about the pups than anyone else. Because of this, they need to communicate to you any information, incidents, or just general issues or concerns that need to be addressed. A great way to facilitate this is to hold periodic staff meetings.

In a meeting, your staff can publicly raise issues that might be bothering them or offer suggestions on how the day care center could improve its operation or image. Perhaps someone wants to discuss a new product that might do well in the retail items showcase or mention a special event that could impact the DDC. There is always plenty to talk about, and suggestions should be welcomed and encouraged. Staff meetings encourage your employees to take more ownership in the day care center, which can only help improve job performance and satisfaction.

The dogs and their "pack behaviors" were constant topics at my staff meetings. How the dogs are behaving with each other is a very important part of dog day care and should always be discussed and improved. Employees can exchange ideas on how to best keep the pack well managed, share effective solutions, and find out about other people's experiences. Often, ideas come out of these staff meetings that foster new procedures and policies. When this happens, you should write up the additional or

modified action and publish it in your policy and procedures manual. This is also a good time to talk about problem dogs who may not be suitable for day care.

Staff meetings are essential for running your DDC. They not only serve as your communication forum, but they reinforce how your employees can work as a team.

Independent Contractors

If you have an independent contractor working at your DDC, such as a freelance groomer or trainer, you'll still need to manage them. This is your business and your reputation on the line, so make sure that they are doing a good job. You have the final say about whether they are working up to your standards.

Veterinarians

Although you won't be hiring a vet to have on call, it's always good to develop a relationship with someone you trust who is close to your DDC. It's not always possible to get a dog to his individual vet, so have someone readily available. I always had a list of veterinarians and their numbers on the wall by the phone.

If you have freelance groomers working at your DDC, you'll need to manage them.

Vendors

For your doggy day care, you will need equipment, supplies, and retail items. (For a sample start-up inventory, see Chapter 5.) You'll depend on vendors and distributors to supply you with these items, and you'll be approached by lots of people who will want your business.

Selecting a Vendor

Selecting a vendor is more important than most people think, and it comes down to trust. Trust that the vendor will be around for the long term; trust that the vendor is reliable in getting you the products you need and on time; and trust that the vendor delivers top-quality products.

One way to find vendors is to ask other business owners for recommendations. While this is a great way to find someone, you also shouldn't be afraid to try a new distributor, who might be able to introduce you to new or more advanced products. New vendors are also anxious to get your business and may offer some substantial discounts to sign you up, as well as freebies to further entice you.

It's up to you to manage your distributor. If she doesn't deliver on time or doesn't meet your expectations, let her know your concerns right away. If there is no improvement after your complaints, drop that vendor for one of her competitors.

Research Products

It's important to stay on top of trends in day care products, so it's up to you to read and research what is available and popular. Use manufacturers' websites and dog care magazines to scout for what's new. You can find out about improved foods, snacks, grooming products, and cleaning supplies—items that you might want to try in your own DDC. Then ask your distributor to get you a sample of the particular item so that you can try it out for your business.

Develop a Good Relationship

I have found it helpful to get to know my vendors. Small things like congratulating them on a wedding or wishing them happy birthday can help build a good relationship. I also gave them a small token gift from time to time to let them know that I appreciated their special interest in my day care business. In the long run, cultivating business relationships will help with the success of your DDC.

Getting in touch with the right vendors will make running your DDC much easier.

Community

Cultivating a good relationship with the community is good for any business, but for doggy day care centers, it is essential. Because doggy day care centers are a relatively new business, some people don't fully understand them and may have a negative impression about them. It's up to you to solve this problem. You want to portray a positive image to your community, and because doggy day care centers help dogs and dog owners, it should be easy. But how can you do this?

You want the community to know that:
1. Your doggy day care business exists.
2. You provide a valuable and needed service to dogs and their owners.

We'll talk more about how to market your DDC in the next chapter, but here are some ideas about how to reach out to your community and enhance the image of your business—with the added bonus of attracting new clients!

Donations

I can't stress enough how important it is for your doggy day care center to have a good image within your town. Donate as generously as you can to town fundraising events for police, firefighters, schools, or any of the charitable campaigns that occur each year in your town. This reinforces the idea that your business is an integral part of the community.

Open House

Consider holding an open house once or twice a year. Get the word out by posting notices at veterinary offices, groomers, and pet stores. And try sending postcard announcements from the list of dog owners you obtained during your feasibility study. Because open houses are usually held on Saturdays or Sundays, you won't be at full capacity. You might ask a few clients (with very well-behaved dogs) to leave their dogs at your DDC for a few hours during the event. Invite dog lovers and families to come for a tour of your facility, and let the adults and children view the dogs. With this audience of local people, take the opportunity to hold an informal question-and-answer session so that all of the attendees understand how your business works and how important it is to the community. As the visitors leave, provide them with a goody bag filled with people snacks, doggy snacks or toys, and a brochure about your center.

Hold a costume contest at your DDC to help build up your reputation in the community.

Fun Events

Holding or participating in fun events can help draw attention to your business, as well as help members of the community get more comfortable with you.

Costume Contest

One of the most fun events we held at my DDC was an annual Halloween costume contest for dogs. We would send out a press release about the costume party to the local newspapers and radio stations to promote the event and to let everyone know that participating dogs needed a current inoculation record and had to be leashed. We took photos of all of the dogs and gave out small prizes for the best costumes. The response was great, and the locals began looking forward to the event each year. Costume contests also provide a chance to get free publicity via a newspaper article.

Participate in Parades

Another way to interact with your community and attract potential clients is to walk with your dogs in any town parades. You and your staff should wear shirts with your business logo on them. Have brochures and business cards ready to hand out. You can even dress up the dogs if so inclined. Showing off your well-behaved, adorable dogs is sure to win over the crowd. It's also a great way to advertise your business and answer any questions about dog day care.

Secret Santa

Sometimes it's important to keep your clients feeling special, as their high opinion of you will definitely be reflected in the community at large. Because your client base can run into the hundreds, it's usually too expensive to buy presents for everyone during special occasions. My solution was to run a Secret Santa gift swap during the holiday season. We made name tags for each dog and hung them on our holiday tree. Each client would pick a name and buy a small gift for the dog. At the end of December, we held the Secret Santa swap. This is a great way make your clientele feel connected.

Administration

By now you should appreciate how important it is to connect with all of the important players who impact your DDC. But there is one additional area you must pay attention to daily: the business operations. Running a successful business requires the ability to handle many different administrative tasks. It's the side of the business that has nothing to do with playing with dogs or managing people—it's the tedious task of recordkeeping. Every business must keep accurate and up-to-date financial records for payroll, tax payments, accounting, and budgeting. You will find that you must keep records of your daily dog census, your employees' work hours, and many other similar tasks.

A good business software program will help you run your DDC efficiently.

Many years ago, this was done manually with accounting ledgers and check stubs. But in today's complex electronic world, it's necessary to use more sophisticated tools to manage your recordkeeping. Luckily, these computer-based programs make administrative tasks much easier for today's DDC owner.

Kennel Software

There are a variety of kennel software programs available that will work for your DDC. Some are more complex than others, so I recommend taking advantage of the free trials that the software companies offer. This will give you the chance to test-drive the software and get comfortable with your options.

Software Functionality

Most of the software packages have all of the capabilities that you would ever need. But it's wise to know your specific application software requirements before you begin your evaluation. Most of these requirements are based on the size of your center and the range of services you will be offering to your customers. Some of the functions included in most software packages include:

- **Accounts payable:** Tracks invoices you owe to various vendors.
- **Accounts receivable:** Tracks money owed and received from customers.
- **Appointments:** Tracks confirmations and check-ins and check-outs.
- **Bookkeeping** (some integrate with QuickBooks): Tracks money taken in and paid out during the time period specified.
- **Employee management:** Area to store employee information for easy contact.
- **Punch cards:** Some DDCs offer discount packages that include punch cards; this feature tracks the punches.
- **Reports:** Creates financial reports for different time periods and criteria.
- **Reservations for grooming, boarding, and daycare:** Tracks exactly who you have checking in or out that day and at what times.
- **Touch screen check in:** Tracks employee hours.
- **Tracking customer information:** Pulls up customer contact information easily.
- **Tracking pets information:** Area to track specifics on any given dogs (e.g., allergies, dog food, vet info).

These are the basic requirements that your software should include. Plus, there are additional features available, such as swipe cards to track the dogs, that you can add on.

Once you understand the particular requirements for your DDC, call the software vendor and ask questions, including:

- What are the features included in each package?
- Is there a one-time set-up fee or continuing monthly maintenance charges?
- What kind of help is available for setting up the system?
- Are manuals and training available?
- Are software updates free, or do you pay each time a new version comes out?
- Does the vendor offer phone support? During what hours?

- Can you contact the vendor by e-mail?
- Does the vendor have references from current customers? Can you speak to the vendor about the system and its company?
- Does the vendor offer a free demo so that you can test before you buy?

Remember, you will be using this software every day, so you need to be comfortable with your choice. After your call with the software company, think about how receptive it was to your questions and concerns. This will give you a clearer understanding of how the company will work with you later as a customer. You should also do your own background check on the company. Check with the Better Business Bureau to see if there have been any negative filings against it.

This software won't include help with running your payroll. For that, hire a payroll service or check out payroll software that's available online. A service may make your life easier, though.

Kennel Software

Below is a list of some of the more popular software companies. This is not meant to be an endorsement of any particular software product but just a way to get you started on your evaluation process. Prices vary according to the package in which you're interested. (Contact the company to find out about any changes or additions since this writing.)

K9 Bytes
www.k9bytessoftware.com
Features: Free data conversion from certain programs.

Kennel Connection
www.kennelconnection.com
Features: Mix and match modules, depending on your needs; free data conversion; discount on software if using another program; free standard support for the first year.

Kennel Link
www.kennellink.com
Features: Internet-based service, so data is backed up nightly on its server; free software upgrades.

Kennel Soft—Atlantis
www.kennelsoft.com
Features: Upgrades and support are free for the first year.

KennelSuite
www.planesoftware.com
Features: Updates are always free; upgrades are free for first year; can convert from another program.

Daily Checklists

For your day-to-day operations, here's a checklist of everything you'll need to do. Make sure that your staff knows exactly what needs to be done for each shift.

Opening

- Pull files for all-day care or overnight dogs.
- Fill water buckets in each room for the dogs.
- Make sure baggies stocked for the day to pick up poop.
- Fill mop bucket with disinfectant and replace mop head.
- Put garbage bag in poop bucket.
- Wipe out all crates.
- Wipe down office and vacuum.
- Feed any boarding dogs.
- Start laundry.
- Fill in "Daily Check-In Tracking Form" as dogs are checked in. (See Appendix: Form 9.)
- Enter each dog's feeding information as they are checked in.
- Gather any belongings of dogs checking out.

During the Day

- Keep floors free of urine and feces.
- Keep mop water clean.
- Feed lunches.
- Do the laundry.
- Enter dogs into the computer and put away files.

- Take care of any baths/grooming/nail trims.
- Take boarding reservations. (For a sample "Bed & Breakfast Reservation Form," see Appendix: Form 10.)
- Label crates of dogs who are boarding.

Closing
- Feed boarding dogs.
- Sweep and mop day care area.
- Wipe out all "time-out" crates.
- Pull next day's reservations.
- Clean front office.
- Do the laundry.
- Put boarding dogs to bed.
- Set alarm.
- Turn out lights.

Stay organized and stay positive, and soon your DDC will be running like a dream!

A Day in the Life

One of the hardest parts of owning a DDC is failing a dog for enrollment. I once failed a 14-year-old Jack Russell Terrier who was very set in his ways. During the interview process, he wanted no part of any of the other dogs—not the ideal candidate for doggy day care, to say the least. Later that day, I had to run over to our local pet supply store. While minding my own business in one of the aisles, I heard someone shouting—behind me stood the woman whose dog I had just failed for enrollment. She was screaming at the top of her lungs, furious that I could've done such a thing to her and her dog! I tried to calm her down, but she would have no part of it. I soon realized that I was not going to get a word in with this emotionally enraged dog owner. By this time, the entire store was watching the scene. Embarrassed, I abruptly left my shopping cart still filled with items and ran out of the store. I can honestly state that was the first time I'd ever been chased out of a pet supply store.

Lesson of the Day: Stick to your guns when you make a decision, no matter how hard it may be. If you start making exceptions for people and dogs with whom you're not comfortable, you will be miserable! Judging from the outburst I witnessed, the Jack Russell's owner was not a client I wanted to deal with on a daily basis. So despite the dramatic scene, it was a good decision not to enroll her dog.

Chapter

8

Marketing and Advertising

Marketing and advertising begin long before you open up your dog day care business—and they never end.

You did some passive marketing while you were gathering information to determine the feasibility of the business and again when researching for your business plan. It occurred simply because you were talking to people about the business—this let them know that there was a prospective DDC coming to their town. When you surveyed veterinary clinics, visited town hall, checked out insurance agencies, and met with contractors, you already started to spread the word about your exciting new business.

Marketing Budget

Remember your business plan from way back in Chapter 3? If you did it correctly, you made sure to budget at least 10% of your annual operating budget for marketing and advertising each year. It should have been a line item in your business plan and should be left there as a budget line item.

But marketing and advertising must be much more proactive. They require networking with other people on a frequent basis. Marketing is not just a scripted text telling people about the business—it takes many forms.

Grand Opening

You will want a lot of attention when you open your new business but not on the very first day you open. Give yourself time to iron out any of the opening wrinkles, which may take a few days or up to a month. Then when you feel comfortable, schedule your "official" grand opening.

Press Release

Create a press release that announces your grand opening. Press releases are a great way to get free advertising, but many people don't take advantage of them because they feel that they can't write a good article. But there is no need to avoid it—most newspapers will write the article themselves if you give them about 10 to 15 minutes for an interview. Go to your local paper's website, and there may even be instructions for submitting a press release for free.

Sample Press Release

Your press release should read something like the following:

On July 1st, [your town] will have a new dog care business located at [business address]. [Name of your business] will provide dog care from 7:00 a.m. to 7:00 p.m. for owners who don't want to leave their dogs alone. The concept of doggy day care centers started on the West Coast many years ago and have become very popular for contemporary dog owners. The facility's owner [your name] has years of experience with all dog breeds. If interested, stop by the facility, visit its website at www.yourwebsite.com, or telephone at xxx-xxx-xxxx.

The press release for your official grand opening should go out about a week before the event. Often you can get a photographer to come and take a photo of your new facility on this special day.

Target a local dog show or agility match to hand out flyers for your business.

Other Ways to Get the Word Out

- Don't forget the radio stations! They will often publicize the opening of a local business and might even provide a few ad-libs that could work in your favor.
- If it's not too costly, consider inserting colorful flyers announcing your grand opening in the local newspaper.
- Send postcards about your grand opening to the list of dog owners that you obtained from your research at town hall back in the feasibility stage.

Websites

The Internet has become one of the best marketing tools for the small business owner because it offers inexpensive advertising and reaches a wide number of people. Most people looking for a DDC—whether they are a new pet owner, relocating from another area, or even coming to your town for a vacation—are much more likely to surf the Internet before opening up the huge tome of yellow pages.

Developing a Website

You can easily develop a website yourself with the plethora of tools available. There are books, Internet hosting sites, and software packages that will help you set up your own website, and you can learn how to show graphics, feature doggy photos, and even upload video. If you need help developing your website, contact a consultant who is familiar with the dog day care business and ideally has owned a center.

If you decide that you don't want to develop your own website, you can hire a webmaster to do the job. But there is a downside to this choice—it's easy to become dependent on this service. You will want to update and modify your site from time to time, and it makes much more sense for you to take care of these small tasks independently rather than call the webmaster back for each modification. This not only becomes costly, but often the web developer doesn't understand exactly what you want.

Website Content

Include the following content on your website:

- Photos of your center, including pictures of your staff doing their jobs, as well as lots of pictures of the dogs.
- Your DDC brochure, preferably in a downloadable format.
- The requirements for admitting dogs into your facility so that any potential client has a clear understanding of your policies and procedures.
- Intake forms (see Appendix: Form 4), preferably in a downloadable format. This way, potential clients can have any paperwork filled out before they come in.
- Photos and text that reinforce how you keep the center clean and the dogs happy.
- Your experience with dogs and understanding of canine behavior—it's what most people will be interested in as they shop around for a doggy day care center.
- An e-mail contact page that enables visitors to submit any questions for you directly from the site.
- A toll-free telephone number. It gives the impression of an established business, and it doesn't cost much.
- A "bulletin board" of scheduled events at the facility.
- Positive testimonials from your clients, which reinforces the professional care that you and your staff provide.
- Links to other dog-related websites (with the understanding that they will link back to you), which increases your credibility and exposure.

Rates and Fees?

The one feature that you should not put on your site is your current rates and fees. This can be argued both ways. But most DDC owners, like you, should want to talk with the prospective client and persuade her that your center is best for her dog. It will be appropriate to discuss your center's rates at that time. Other owners put the rates on the site. If the visitor thinks them a bit high, she will never call you. It also leaves you open to competitive facilities. If you can't talk with the dog owner, I often think that the DDC owner has missed an opportunity to convince the client that your dog day care center is in her best interest.

Printed Material

Handing out various types of printed material, like business cards and brochures, can help get the word out about your DDC.

Business Cards

Designing your business card should not be taken lightly—a lot can be determined simply by looking at a person's business card. Your business card should include:

- your DDC logo
- your business name
- your name (e.g., Jane Doe, owner/operator)
- business address
- phone/fax numbers
- e-mail address
- website URL
- incentive printed on the back, such as 10% discount or a free bath, etc. (optional)

The logo should stand out on the business card, along with your business name. At the same time, the card should not look too busy or overwhelming. I suggest that you use good-quality stock for your cards. Good rag-bond material makes a much better impression than the typical flimsy desktop printing stock.

The important thing to realize is that these cards don't get handed out on their own. Distribute small bundles of them at key locations, such as veterinary clinics, pet supply stores, dog groomers, supermarkets, and other local stores that allow public posting of cards. And above all, always carry a few business cards on you. You'll be amazed how many business cards you'll hand out just by meeting new people in your everyday life.

Brochures

You should create a brochure for your DDC that describes all of the services you offer. You may not always have time to describe your facility in detail when people walk in off the street. If you have a brochure, you can give it to the potential client to look over and then make an appointment to discuss your business further.

Your brochure can be as simple or as creative as you like. There are many software programs that can help you design it yourself, or you can hire a graphic artist to create it for you. It all depends on your budget.

Your brochure should include:

Front Cover
- name of your business and logo
- contact information, including address, phone, e-mail, and website

Inside
- importance of doggy day care—what it's all about
- your mission statement
- services you offer, including grooming, training, boarding, retail
- about you and your staff
- about the facility
- hours of operation
- interview process
- criteria for admission
- directions
- contact information (repeated)

Like your business cards, brochures are a great marketing piece to leave at other local dog-related businesses. Keep a handful in your car (along with your business cards) to hand out to people when you're not at the day care.

Letterhead

A nice touch for your business is to design letterhead with your logo and business address at the top. Use it for all of your correspondence.

Networking Groups

Networking groups, which help you meet other businesspeople in your town, are a great way to build your business. Usually, it's a local group with one representative from each type of local business. These groups are a good way to pass referrals and build relationships in your town. Within this group you can promote yourself to many other like-minded businesspeople, who will in turn refer your business. It is said that everyone within their sphere knows 200 people, and they in turn know 200, and so on—that's a lot of people and a lot of referrals. And joining a networking group shows that you are an ambitious business owner serious about building the business. Just look up "networking groups" for your area online to find one near you.

More Marketing Ideas

Use your imagination to come up with creative ideas to market your DDC. Here are a few of my favorites.

T-Shirts

I don't know why, but I'm compelled to read the text on every T-shirt I see, whether it's a political joke, a cute saying, or an advertisement for a company. I find that most people have the same habit. Have colorful T-shirts made up with your logo, website, and phone number. Try to "hook" people into calling your day care by asking a leading question, like "Does your dog care? Call xxx-xxx-xxxx to find out" or "Where would your dog rather be today? Call me at xxx-xxx-xxxx."

These T-shirts will be a financial loss leader—you give them out free, so you won't be making any money off of them. But it's free advertising for you whenever someone wears it. Give them out to your clients, friends, and the general public at dog shows, competitions, and carnivals.

Staff members should also wear the T-shirts as their uniform, and you can encourage them to wear them out in public—what better publicity?

Flyers

If you attend dog events, try bringing some colorful flyers about your DDC to put on car windshields. I know that many people find them annoying, but you can bet they always read them when they must remove them from underneath the windshield wipers. However, you must check with your town to see if there are any regulations about placing flyers on vehicle windows. If it's prohibited, you could always hand them out personally at the events.

The flyer should have your logo, name of your business, and contact information—address and telephone number. Plus, you should add some sort of incentive to the person reading it. For example, offer a free day of day care if accepted, a free screening process, or a free bag of dog food to the first 25 people who respond. You can use your creativity here—everyone loves free stuff!

Be a Sponsor

A great way to advertise your business is to sponsor an athletic team. There are plenty of choices, including children's little league baseball, basketball, soccer, etc. And don't forget your town's festive holiday parade. You can likely sponsor a float that rolls down Main Street, with your DDC's banner and some of your best-looking dogs on top of the float.

Radio

As a business owner, you may be invited on a radio or Internet talk show for an interview. After a few questions about your business, the host will usually open the phone lines for listeners to call in and ask you about specific doggy day care questions. This can be great advertising for you and a lot of fun!

Send Out Cards

I use the online service Send Out Cards for my marketing. You can upload your logo and photos of client's dogs to create customized cards that the service will send out for you. You can track your client's birthdays and send gifts to your clients on special occasions. It adds a nice personal touch to your business.

Word of Mouth

The old business adage "Word of mouth is the best advertising" holds true for your doggy day care. If you can keep your clients happy (by keeping their dogs happy), they will advertise for you. They'll be proud to recommend your business, which is the best way to gain new clients. Don't ever underestimate the importance of simply running a good business—that will always be your best advertising.

Marketing and advertising are necessary for the health of your doggy day care business, and they're easier than you think—just use some of the creative methods listed in this chapter, or brainstorm your own creative ideas.

A Day in the Life

Before I started my own DDC, I really had no idea how well word of mouth worked, especially in the care-giving field. One afternoon, I sent a couple of my employees down to a dog show that was happening in town to hand out flyers. A couple from out of state stopped by the DDC and introduced their dog to us. He soon became a welcome addition to our DDC family whenever he was in town. That couple then recommended my facility to three other couples who traveled in our area with their dogs, and we got a nice bit of business out of it.

Lesson of the Day: You never know who is going recommend your business, so keep up the marketing initiatives!

Chapter

9

Q & A: Running a Doggy Day Care Center

We've discussed how to start and manage your doggy day care center. In this chapter, I wanted to touch on a few issues that will inevitably pop up while you're operating your business.

These are questions I get asked all the time as a consultant. While you may not like all of my answers, they come from my years of experience. They're intended to give you some focused insight about running your business and will hopefully allow you to avoid common problems and pitfalls.

Managing the Dogs

Q: What takes place during the dog screening and dog owner interviews?

A: You (and your manager, if you have one) should sit down with the dog owner and discuss how your DDC runs. Emphasize that not all of the dogs can acclimate to a doggy day care center because adapting to a "pack mentality" isn't for every dog. This is especially true of adult dogs who have been left alone in the home for several years.

Try to get a good sense of the potential client—how she interacts with her dog and with the staff. Even if you like the dog and want to accept him, if the owner's personality seems like it won't mesh with yours, pass on the application. Demand for dog day care is high, and you can afford to be selective to make life easier for you and your staff.

When you screen the dog, take him out of the owner's physical company. There can be no outside influence during this process—dogs, like kids, behave differently when they are on their own. Look at the dog's personality. Observe how playful he is (or isn't). Look for aggressiveness by playing with the pooch, and watch his reactions to your movements. Inspect him for cleanliness, tick and flea infestation, or any signs of infectious diseases. Introduce the dog to a small group of dogs.

During the screening process, supervise an introduction to another dog.

I declined more than 300 applicants in just three years because the dog or the owner failed my screening. The more thorough and rigid you are during the screening interviews, the more manageable your dogs and clients will be.

Remember—screening is everything!

Q: What inoculations must be current before enrolling a dog?

A: The required vaccinations are:

- distemper
- rabies
- Bordetella (kennel cough)
- negative fecal test (proof on no internal parasites or worms)
- flea/tick program
- heartworm prevention

Your client must present proof of these things before her dog is allowed to join the DDC.

Q: Should I accept unneutered or unspayed adult dogs?

A: You can accept young puppies who are still intact, but they must be neutered or spayed after seven months. Any intact dogs older then seven months should not be accepted—no exceptions.

Q: Should I place age restrictions on the dogs I accept?

A: Puppies should be at least over 12 weeks old and through his puppy shots. Other than that, I had no age restrictions. I loved having senior dogs at my facility, and I believed that it was good for them to get some stimulation from other dogs. It's always helpful to have an area where the older (or even very mellow) dogs can go to rest from the more exuberant dogs.

Q: Are there any breeds that I should not accept at my DDC?

A: This is a controversial subject and a hard choice for a true dog lover. Unfortunately, pit bull-type breeds have a bad reputation, and some areas even have legislation that bans them. I'm not biased against these types of dogs, but I've found that many dog owners don't want their pup in the same mix with them. Also, accepting certain breeds may cause your insurance payments to go up or even be canceled. So for purely business reasons, I did not accept them. It kept the peace and prevented insurance issues. In the end, the choice is up to you.

Q: How should I introduce a new dog to my facility?

A: If the dog has passed your initial interview process, ask his owner to drop him off especially early on his first day. If the newcomer enters your DDC while all of the enrolled dogs are already present, the entire pack will approach him at once—and chaos is sure to ensue. If he's there first, he'll be the "sniffer" and not the "sniffee." This makes for a more controlled and managed introduction.

Q: What are the signs a dog is anxious or nervous and might instigate a confrontation?

A: Dogs are individuals and will give different signals for how they are feeling. However, there are some general signs to look for, such as the hackles quickly rising, showing teeth with a subdued growl, heavy panting, foaming at the mouth, and an overall nervous demeanor. If a dog is overly fearful and anxious, he may "fear bite." It won't take you long to be able to quickly spot signs of trouble, especially when dogs are approaching each other. The tensest moments are usually the introductions, and once they are over, it will become easier for everyone.

Q: How long does it take for a dog to acclimate to the doggy day care environment?

A: There really isn't one answer to this question. Some dogs acclimate within a day, while others can take more than a week. And unfortunately, some never make the transition. Just remember not to accept any dog who behaves badly in the pack environment.

Q: Do some dogs gravitate toward certain dogs and not others?

A: This might sound funny, but I always noticed how cliques developed among the dogs. Dogs would stay together with their friends and not integrate with other groups. Often, those who came together at the opening of the facility stayed together for years after they first met. Also, it sometimes happens that dogs of the same breed tend to like each other's company.

Some dogs naturally gravitate towards each other, and become "day care buddies."

Q: Are water hoses effective in discouraging persistent mounting and fighting?

A: Water hoses are useful; however, in my experience, spray bottles were used more often. They are more portable than hoses and usually do the trick.

Q: You mentioned in an earlier chapter that your DDC was taking in around 50 dogs per day. If everyone was dropping off and picking up at the same time, how did you keep it organized?

A: Well, that was a trick! The majority of our customers dropped off between 7:30 a.m. and 8:30 a.m. and picked up from 5:00 p.m. to 6:00 p.m. Make sure that you have adequate staffing during these times. During the morning drop-off, you will find that the dogs can't wait to get back to the play area with all of their friends. You will not only need someone to bring the dogs from the entrance to the day care room but also a staff member located inside the room to welcome the dogs and make for a smooth transition. Excitement can escalate into a scuffle very quickly, so it's important that someone from your staff is in the room keeping the dogs calm.

Make sure you have adequate staffing during you main drop off times.

The evening pickup can be tricky. Take the leash the owner gives you when picking up and leash the dog before he enters the lobby. This will ensure that there are no escapes because the front door is constantly opening with other owners picking up their dogs. Your and your staff need to be careful during this time—the dogs will be excited to see their owners but are also in a protective mode as well. Never let two dogs out into the lobby at the same time. On more than one occasion at my DDC, the dogs became overly protective of their space (and that includes your lobby) as well as of their owners, and fights broke out between dogs who had been playing together nicely all day.

Managing the Clients

Q: *What questions or issues do most clients have after their dogs are enrolled in a doggy day care center?*

A: They tend to only be interested in knowing how happy their dog was during the day. They usually don't want to hear bad news, like he was aggressive. However, you have to be prepared to be honest at all times, even if it stings a little bit. The owner will appreciate it, and it shows that you are aware of what is going on in your day care. They'll usually ask if he played, took a nap, ate, etc., so be prepared at the end of each day to chat a bit with the owners. Part of your business will be interacting with the pet parents and keeping them up to speed on how their dog is doing.

Q: *What's the most effective tool to keeping the dog owners happy?*

A: Pay attention to your clients (just as you do their dogs). Try setting up a "Dog Owners' Suggestion Box" in your lobby. Clients can submit their ideas (anonymously or otherwise). Learning about their ideas is helpful, and if the suggestion makes sense you can implement it.

You can also hold special events for your clients and dogs to participate in together. We held Halloween parties and contests of all kinds. These events, in addition to the "Doggy of the Month" award, are things your clients are bound to respond to.

It's essential to demonstrate to your clients that you are not in the DDC business just for the money but because you love dogs too.

Q: *In a busy DDC, how do I communicate with my clients?*

A: Make it a point to meet and greet your clients every morning. During evening pickups, take a few minutes to discuss how the day went for each pooch. Try to emphasize the positive character of the dog—owners like to hear that type of information.

You can also create a monthly newsletter. It can be brief but should outline any upcoming events (and make sure to include your "Doggy of the Month"). You can also use it as an opportunity to inform owners about what's going on with your staff.

Your staff should be capable and willing to do all parts of the job—even the less fun tasks, like clean up.

Managing the Staff

Q: You mentioned how important it is to hire good staff, but what exactly should I look for?

A: The first thing you need to look for when hiring is the applicant's unwavering confidence in working with a pack of many different dog breeds. If there is even a slight inclination of fear, you can be sure that staff member won't work out. The ideal staff member has a calm but assertive demeanor with dogs.

One other important thing to look for is if the person is capable and willing to do all of the unattractive, less fun tasks that are part of the job.

Q: How can I motivate my DDC staff?

A: Remember, your staff members are people too! Everyone needs a breather, so try to be generous by giving breaks every few hours. Encouraged them to get away from the dogs and spend time in the employee lounge or outside.

If a staff member is interested in a dog-related career, such as trainer, groomer, or vet tech, encourage her to take self-study courses for certification. If the employee is serious and it's within your budget, you might offer to pay for the small expenses for the courses and examinations.

As I mentioned in Chapter 7, be sure to hold staff meetings. This gives employees a sense of belonging to the business. Giving them an opportunity to recommend new ideas and have a say in the course of the business goes a long way in motivating people.

Provide them with company shirts as part of their uniform while on duty. It makes them feel like part of a team and demonstrates a more professional atmosphere.

When you have a happy staff, you'll have happy dogs, and ultimately, happy dog owners.

Doggy day cares are increasing in popularity all around the country.

Q: Should I offer health insurance to my staff?

A: Offering health insurance is required in some areas. But even if it's not legally required, I think to get quality people who are going to stick with you, you should offer these benefits after a certain trial period.

If possible, offer your staff health care benefits.

Looking to the Future

Q: Do you think doggy day cares will continue to grow, or are they just a flash in the pan?

A: In my personal opinion, day cares are here to stay and will only get bigger and better. Dogs still reign as man's best friend and will continue to do so for the foreseeable future. Unlike decades ago, dogs are now considered members of the family. As such, more and more owners are feeling guilty about the time their dogs spend alone. Most pet owners I know say that they would go into debt if the health and safety of their pet depended on it. And the amount of money spent on dog care and dog amenities continues to grow. Doggy day care is just one more opportunity for dog owners to ensure that their dog is given professional care while they are apart.

Q: Are there any official regulations regarding the running of a doggy day care? Why would I need these kinds of rules for running my business?

A: Since this pet care service started on the West Coast, it has spread quickly over many urban and rural areas in the United States and Canada. As it becomes more prevalent, there will be more regulatory guidelines developed for this pet care business. I believe that this will only help the industry.

I personally have promoted the need for more regulations to my state's legislature. The regulatory guidelines I'm fighting for will ensure that the DDC business is run by professional pet care providers. The last thing anyone wants is to have doggy day care centers run by unknowledgeable, uncaring people. It's catastrophic for the well-being of the dogs and creates a negative image of the business in general.

Putting statutory protections in place legitimizes the industry. These regulations need not be restrictive but should focus on the safety and protection of the dogs. Most laws will cover things like the minimum amount of space needed and the proper temperature controls inside and outside for the animals. They will also subject DDCs to periodic inspections to ensure cleanliness of the facility and safety of the dogs.

Q: Is there a way to certify staff working at my DDC?

A: Right now, no. I'm hoping this is another area that comes under regulation. I would love to see mandatory exams after 90 days of job training for anyone who works at a DDC. The exam would test the person's knowledge and ability to care for all types of breeds in a pack environment. It would test their ability to react properly with the dogs under duress. They would receive state certification upon successfully passing the exam. Copies of these certificates would be displayed in the reception area for dog owners to view. Should staff members fail the exam, they would be prevented from returning to work until they passed it during a retake process.

The certification would also help staff members who apply for a new position in the future. They could take the well-deserved certification with them should they relocate to other states.

Q: Are there any needs that current DDCs are not serving that my facility might be able to fill?

A: There is a serious issue I see that is not currently addressed by anyone in the industry: dogs who, through no fault of their own, are homeless. I'm speaking specifically about the death of an owner or seniors who are unable to care for their dogs on a daily basis. Perhaps because this is a sad topic, no one wants to think about it.

If there is no family willing to take on the pets in these situations, the poor dogs are assigned to shelters and often euthanized. I believe that doggy day care centers can offer a helpful service in these cases.

One option is for the elderly dog owner to pay for the DDC to care for her dog while she is living in a nursing home. Most nursing homes allow visits from pets, so the DDC owner can arrange for the dog to visit his owner at the nursing home periodically. This will lift the spirits of both the owner and the beloved dog.

Another option is for dog owners to purchase long-term pet care for their dog in advance of any terminal illness. The owner will know that her pet is living a happy life with appropriate care. The DDC can provide the care in conjunction with a pet-adoption service, which gives the pooch a second chance with a new, loving owner.

Although doggy day care businesses are skyrocketing in popularity, you shouldn't overlook other potential dog care business,

Part II

Other Dog Care Businesses: Dog Sitting, Dog Walking, and Dog Camps

such as dog sitting or dog walking. They are both burgeoning enterprises that don't require as many start-up costs as a doggy day care business.

Chapter

10

Starting a Dog Sitting Business

With more than 63 million homes that have at least one pet, starting your own dog sitting business is appealing.

Historically, pet sitting had been relegated to relatives, youngsters, teenagers, or college students on a short-term basis for a bit of pocket money. But today, there are thousands of people who provide pet sitting services on a full-time basis and make a comfortable living doing so.

What Is Dog Sitting?

People today have busy lives, and the time available to care for their dogs is limited. Many dog owners can't get home during the day to let their dog out for a bathroom break and some exercise. Some people travel a lot or are away in the evenings and unable to feed or let their dogs out.

That's where dog sitters come in—they come into the home and take care of the dog when the owners can't. Services can include feeding, walking, and playing with the dogs. Dog sitters may also perform other house sitting duties, such as watering plants, taking in the mail, and light house cleaning, but interacting with the dog is always the priority.

Dog owners who work away from the home all day may need a dog sitter to help care for their dogs.

Who Needs Dog Sitters?

In Part I, we discussed the typical dog owner who is away all day at the workplace and has a need for a dog day care center each workday of the month. However, not all dogs are accepted into a DDC. Many dogs fail the interview test during the application process and are not accepted for enrollment. So what's an owner to do? She may come to realize that the next best thing is to have someone sit with her dog for a period of time in the home.

There are other dog owners who don't want their dog put in a new environment—they'd prefer to have the dog remain in his own home with familiar surroundings. This happens frequently with older dogs. Let's face it, changing environments is as stressful for dogs as it is for humans. Many owners feel more comfortable knowing that their dog is safe at home and not confronted with a different environment with multiple dogs and diluted attention.

There is also a segment of dog owners who just can't afford the cost of daily dog care facilities. If the expense of a day care center doesn't fit into the budget, home dog sitting can be a comfortable compromise for the dog owner.

In addition, one of the biggest reasons a dog owner needs a pet sitter is travel. Although airlines and railroads have become a bit more flexible in allowing pets to travel, many owners know that it may not be the best thing for their dog. It can be uncomfortable and scary, especially with the strange noises, temperature variations, and break from the dog's typical routine. Some people even go so far as to cancel their vacations because of the stress it puts on the dogs while they are away. This makes many dog owners open to the idea of in-home pet sitting to take care of their dog while they must travel.

National Organizations

There are several national organizations relating to pet sitters, including Pet Sitters International (PSI), www.petsit.com and the National Association of Professional Pet Sitters (NAPPS), www.petsitters.org. You can find lots of great information about the business on these sites. I think that it is important to join at least one of these organizations—it shows your clients you are serious about your business and have taken the time to learn and stay updated on what is going on in the pet sitting world.

Are You Ready?

There is one point I want to underscore about starting a dog sitting business (or any dog care business, for that matter)—it should never be taken lightly. You need to be in it for the long run—nurturing it and keeping it running not only for yourself but for the dogs and their owners. If you decide to suddenly quit to pursue another job, you'll be upsetting the dog's established routine and leaving your clients in the lurch. So if you are considering embarking on a pet sitting business, commit to it for two to three years, minimum. This will give you time to grow your business and develop a backup plan if you cannot provide your services in the future.

Dog Care Experience

Most people who get into a small dog care business have had a measure of experience either dog sitting or dog walking. You should also have a love of dogs, along with the desire to see the dogs as physically and emotionally comfortable as possible.

If you feel that you need more experience before you jump into the business, ask your friends and relatives if you can dog sit for them. Be up front and tell the dog owners why you are volunteering your time and talent to do this. Don't charge them for the service

and they will jump at the opportunity—they may even end
up your first clients!

Experience is always the best teacher. During this trial
period, you will learn about some of the challenges of the
business, create your own solutions, and learn techniques that will make you more at ease.
After this trial period, you should know if you are cut out for this service.

Plus, if you do complete a trial period with friends and relatives, you'll be able to give
references about your experience—a question that will inevitably come up during initial
interviews with interested clients. (For more on client interviews, see Chapter 11.)

Start-Up

The good news about business planning for a pet sitting business is that the capital
investment is very low—almost negligible—and usually doesn't require developing a
detailed business plan. Because there's usually no need to borrow money, financial risk
doesn't factor into the implementation of the business.

However, it doesn't hurt to consult with other people who have experience in the pet
sitting business (preferably outside of your local area to avoid direct competition). Search
the Internet, and contact pet sitters in different parts of the country. Many will be willing to
help and explain any pitfalls to avoid when starting up.

Feasibility Study

Although starting a pet sitting business is certainly not as complicated as a DDC, you'll still need to do some effective strategic planning, including a feasibility study. (For a detailed description of a feasibility study, see Chapter 2.) You'll need to scope out the opportunities for your dog sitting business to flourish. First, define your territory. You'll want clients near your own home because travel time comes at a premium—keep it as minimal as possible. Delineate your target area on a local street map. Make it fairly large because you don't know the dog population at this point, and only a fraction will want dog care services. The target area can be as small as 25 square miles (40 sq km) to more than 50 square miles (80 sq km). It all depends on the density of the population and the street network in your area. You'll begin to refine your target area as you sign up new clients (trying to make it narrower rather than wider).

Next, determine the census of dogs in this area. As we discussed in Chapter 2, the town hall, veterinary offices, pet supply stores, groomers, and other venues can help roughly determine the number of local dogs. If you feel that there are not enough dogs in the area in which you are looking, you can either expand that area or target another area. If you develop a good relationship with veterinarians or pet store owners, they can give you leads about where the critical mass of dogs can be found.

If you've determined that there are enough dogs to support your business, do your best to try to stay in the target geographical area so that you're not driving from one town to the other. If you can keep the majority of your client's homes in close proximity, you will not only save on travel, but your ability to provide services to more clientele will be enhanced.

Consultants

Consider hiring a consultant or coach to get you started on the right track. It often helps to have a mentor during your initiation to the pet sitting business. You'll be much more prepared, and as the old cliché goes, "Fail to prepare, prepare to fail."

Competition

During the start-up planning process, you must learn how many competitive businesses you'll be up against. One again, go to pet-related businesses in the area (like pet stores and veterinary offices) and ask around or look for flyers. Consult the yellow pages and the Internet to find out if and where there are pet sitting providers in your immediate area. There will undoubtedly be some small setups run by teenagers or part-timers, but you are only interested in learning about businesses professionally run by qualified dog care enthusiasts.

While researching the competition, you might want to call them and find out:
- what hours they are available
- how many dogs they care for

You'll need a reliable vehicle to get to your dog sitting appointments.

- if they have a contract with clients
- what the daily rates are
- what other services they offer
- if they are insured/bonded

The answers to these questions will help you form the parameters of your own pet sitting business and will give you an idea of what the competitive dog care landscape looks like. You may also get ideas for services not currently offered by the competition.

Start-Up Costs

There will be some up-front costs to starting your pet sitting business. Some of these items you probably already have (e.g., computer, printer), while others will be dedicated solely to your new business. You will need to spend money on the following:

- advertising (e.g., flyers, newspaper, radio, etc.)
- business cards
- cell phones for emergencies
- computer
- insurance/bonding premiums (see below)
- office supplies
- printer
- reliable vehicle
- separate phone line for the business
- travel expenses (gasoline)

In addition to these costs, you'll need a box of dog-related "tools" to carry in your car so that you are prepared for any occasion. These include:

- bottled water
- leashes
- poop bags
- pooper scooper
- treats
- water bowl

When you are dog sitting, the owner will most likely have a certain collar or harness for her dog, as well as a leash, but you should still have extras of these items just in case.

Ideally, you will have saved up several hundred dollars to cover these costs, so they can come directly from your out-of-pocket expenses. However, if you don't have any personal resources or any financial capital, you will need to seek outside funding. If this is the case, go through the business planning process described in Part I of this book. Luckily, the amount of planning required is much less than when beginning a DDC. As I mentioned in that section, I highly recommend using free business consulting resources, such as those offered by your local Service Corps of Retired Executives (SCORE) chapter. It's an incredibly valuable resource in case you need to present your funding needs to a bank or lending institution.

Collar Tip

Before you take out any new dog, make sure that his collar is properly fitted and that he is unable to slip out of it.

But if you can support your start-up business without borrowing any funds, you will be much better off. Starting up your pet sitting business will be trying both physically and emotionally, and paying off a business loan can be difficult.

Insurance and Bonding

Unfortunately, we live in a society with unscrupulous service providers and homeowners. Your pet sitting business involves you coming into your client's house alone (except for the dog, of course!) and sometimes staying overnight. Bad things can happen, including missing or damaged items, which may or may not have been your fault. To protect yourself from potential lawsuits, you're going to need liability insurance.

You can be sued for negligence, property damage, and everything in between. Most of the times these claims have no merit, but the cost of hiring an attorney can be significant.

To protect yourself and your business, get proper insurance coverage.

If you've hired an attorney or consultant to help you with any part of the start-up, you may want to ask them for help finding the best coverage. There are various insurance options to choose from, but I've found that Pet Sitters International (PSI) and the National Association of Professional Pet Sitters (NAPPS) are able to provide discounts through various insurers for general liability coverage, which can protect you while you are in the client's home, your own home, or in transit. Their websites can   direct you to the right insurance plans, and you can find out estimated costs for the coverage you need.

Some pet sitters also choose to become legally bonded. This is usually only necessary when you have hired employees, as bonding basically protects you in case of employee theft. (If you are the only employee, there's not much chance you'll be stealing from your clients and putting your business in jeopardy!) I strongly suggest that you study the policies of the bonding organization carefully. Understand what protection you are going to have before you buy it. Like insurance policies, there are a variety of coverage programs, and both the PSI and NAPPS offer bonding. Some pet sitters choose to get

A pet sitting business involves spending time in your client's house alone, so proper insurance is essential.

bonded simply as a marketing tool, even if they don't have any employees. To many clients, saying "fully insured and bonded" sounds pretty good! It gives them confidence in hiring you and makes them feel more comfortable welcoming you into their home while they are away.

Determining Rates and Fees

Before we get into detailed pricing, you must determine which services your pet sitting business will offer. Some clients may be surprised at the current rates for dog sitting. They'll probably compare your rates with dog kennels during your initial interview. You should be prepared to defend your rates compared to the services provided by traditional kennels.

Explain the comparative treatment of the dog cared for in the home versus dropping him off at a low-priced kennel. When a dog is dropped off at a kennel, he is immediately taken to a crate of some type. The amount of time he is let out of the crate will be limited to bathroom breaks. Sometimes the dog is walked briefly for exercise, but this is not done in all cases. Most importantly, there is hardly any quiet time for him—a dog kennel is not a peaceful place conducive to healthy sleep and rest. With dogs barking incessantly, the tired pet never gets a good night's sleep.

Using a pet sitter to come to the home is not only more convenient, but many more services can be offered to the client. You will normally be taking the dog out twice a day to give him exercise and playtime, refresh his water bowl, clean up after him, and give any medications as needed. The dog will not be competing with other dogs hour after hour, and staying at home allows for a familiar and peaceful environment. In addition, you can offer to pick up mail, adjust lighting, take out the trash, and perform light household chores while spending time with the dog.

Workman's Comp

It is wise to have a workman's compensation policy for you and your employees in case of bodily injury, such as a dog bite. This insurance is often mandated in most states.

Emphasize that your alternative to boarding at a dog kennel is a clear stress reliever for clients. They know that while they are away (either for the day or an extended period), their dog is going to be safe, clean, and cared for in the comfort of their own home.

Also, stress that the late fees are not as rigid as with a kennel. Some kennels will charge for an entire extra day if the owner is a mere half hour late picking up the pet. Your potential clients will soon realize that the advantages of your service far outweigh those of the traditional kennel.

In-Home Pet Visits

There's a wide range of rates for pet sitting, depending on your location and the services you'll offer. During your feasibility study, you should have gotten a feel for how much these types of services cost in your area. Also factor in your driving time, mileage, and gas when determining your rates.

Most pet-sitting businesses charge a fee based on a half-hour visit. If there is more than one dog per home, you can (and should) increase the rate, but offer a discount on the additional pet(s). You will find that many clients would like you to come twice a day. If so, consider a discount for that scenario.

If you are offering other services, such as taking the dog to a vet or groomer, charge for the round-trip time it takes to make these visits. Always keep in mind that this is your business, and your services should be compensated justly.

Accounting Note

Keep good records of your travel time when going to a client's house. It is a business expense and must be included when you or your bookkeeper runs your profit and loss accounting statement. This is also a tax write-off—one of the benefits of having your own business.

Pet sitting involves taking the dog out for some exercise and play.

Overnight Pet Sitting

Business travel or vacations will often take owners away from their pets for an extended period, and overnight pet sitting is becoming more popular. Your per-night pricing will vary depending on where you live and the demand for your service. Your price should include several walks, feedings, and of course, lots of TLC!

Consider offering additional house sitting-type services, such as adjusting lighting, taking in the mail or newspaper, etc., to give the overall feel that someone is staying in the home.

Marketing and Advertising

If you have the money, you can advertise your pet sitting business in your local newspaper. However, there are many other inexpensive and effective ways to market your business.

Cold-Calling

During your feasibility study, you may gain access to dog owners' phone numbers from the town hall. If so, consider dedicating several nights to telephone solicitations. Cold-calling is not fun, but it can be productive, and your call just might solve some dog owner's dilemma. Keep your street map by your side as you make each call. When you talk to each dog owner, tell them the purpose of your call and ask if there is any interest in your pet sitting services. If so, make an appointment to meet the owner and the dog.

Business Cards

Your business cards are your calling cards and need to leave a good impression when you give them out. (See Chapter 8 for detailed instructions on designing your business card.) Be sure to carry them on you at all times, whether in a business or social setting. You never know who may be interested in your business, so always offer to give your card to new people you meet.

Flyers

Flyers are probably the best way to advertise your pet sitting business and solicit clients. The flyer should explain the purpose of your business, the services you are offering, a bit about your experience as a dog handler (optional), and of course, your telephone number. Consider including a discount coupon for the first visit to entice people to call you.

- Post flyers at various pet-related businesses, such as veterinary offices, pet stores, etc.
- Perhaps visit your local hospital. Patients may be recovering or in rehab for weeks, and many of them may have no family or neighbors to care for their dogs. Ask the hospital administration if you could post your flyers at predetermined points within the facility. Although the assignment may only be for a short time, these engagements often turn into long-term business relationships.
- Retirement communities that are restricted to elderly people with no children could also be a great potential source of prospective clients. Ask at the front desk if you could leave your flyers out or on a bulletin board.
- Don't forget to pay a visit to the local dog shelter. Many of these dogs are adopted by caring and sensitive owners who can use your services. Make sure that the shelter has your flyers and business cards to hand out to adopting dog owners.

The Business Name

You need to come up with a catchy name for your pet sitting business. Refer back to Chapter 3 for ideas on selecting a business name. Make sure that the name you choose is unique. You can check online for a database of business names to make certain the one you have in mind has not been used. After you select the name (and if you choose to), develop a logo and print up business cards, flyers, letterhead stationary, and brochures. All of these items should have your branding on them.

Websites

I often get asked by prospective pet sitters if they need a website to advertise their services. Because dog sitting services are strictly local, a website isn't a necessity. However, creating one that specifies your geographic area of service certainly doesn't hurt and can give the impression of a stable business.

It is always best to try to develop your own website without relying on

professional website developers. Creating your own site using a template is much easier than you think—there are literally hundreds of software programs to assist you. You can then edit the text any way you want and upload your digital photos. You can make changes as you see fit without incurring the charges that come with hiring someone. This approach reduces the capital cost of hiring a webmaster and eliminates the continuous costs of maintaining the site.

If you do decide to create a website, it should only have the basic essentials of your dog sitting business and the services you provide. As I mentioned with dog day care centers, don't list your fee structure on the website. If the web surfer is sincerely interested, she can call you. But remember, "www" stands for "World Wide Web," so don't be surprised to get calls from people not logistically close to you and who won't turn out to be viable clients.

It is easy to send people to visit your website, so make sure that it is printed on all of your marketing material, including business cards, letterhead, etc.

Be creative! come up with a name, logo and tag line for your business.

HomeDoggie
The Best Care for Your Dog When You Can't Be There

During the process of setting up your pet sitting business, don't forget to consider your long-term goals. You will probably start out as a one-person service provider, but the options to expand are limitless. With the incredible growth of all types of dog care businesses, especially in urban areas, you may find yourself hiring additional staff to meet the escalating demand for your services. Some pet sitters eventually end up doing nothing but the scheduling, marketing, and administrative work for the business they once started all by themselves.

DDCs

As I mentioned earlier, not all dogs are accepted into DDCs. If there is a doggy day care center in your area, you might pay it a visit and (sensitively) find out the names of owners whose dogs were rejected because of their social incompatibility.

A Day in the Life

My very first pet sitting job was spending a week with a beautiful Cavalier King Charles Spaniel named Daisy, whose owners were going away. I met with the clients and took all of the pertinent information, such as contact information and my instructions for Daisy's routine care. They gave me a house key and I left for the night, as they were going on vacation the next morning.

The next day, I pulled up to the house and saw Daisy in the window, obviously happy to see me. I gathered up my things and headed to the door, where Daisy was barking away and scratching to get to me. I put the key in the lock, and—you guessed it—the key wouldn't turn! I hadn't thought to ask for a spare and didn't know if any of their friends or neighbors had access to an extra key. Luckily, I found an open window to the basement and managed to get in.

Lesson of the Day: *Ask your clients to leave a spare key either with their neighbors or hidden somewhere outside, and try the key before you leave their homes.*

Chapter

11

Operating Your Dog Sitting Business

Now that you know how easy it can be to set up your own dog sitting business, let's discuss some of the important issues about this type of dog care.

The Initial Interview

So you've generated interest in your dog sitting business and have some potential clients lined up. Now it's time to schedule the interview. This initial application interview is critically important, and you must be thoroughly prepared. This is not a one-way interview—you and the potential client will be interviewing each other. You need to get a feel for the chemistry between you and the client, and this is also the time to find out how the dog reacts and interacts with you.

Don't Make Snap Decisions

The first thing you should make clear during the interview is that no contractual decisions will be made at this initial meeting. You need to give yourself the option of considering everything you learned during the interview and then politely calling back to either accept or turn down the assignment. Take your time in deciding the clients and dogs you'll be taking on—even if the dog belongs to a relative or friend.

During the initial interview, ask for a tour of the home.

Services Provided

Next, discuss the number of visits per week and the length of time per visit. Also, discuss what is expected during the pet sitting session, including playing, feeding, letting the dog outside, going for a walk, and refreshing his water. Ask for a brief tour of the home (or at least the areas related to the job), and discuss any additional services, such as the light chores mentioned in Chapter 10. Again, this is for informational purposes—you are not agreeing to do anything at this point.

The Dog

While the interview is taking place, you should play with the dog (in a subtle manner, if possible). It is paramount that you feel comfortable and that there is good chemistry between you and the dog. You should feel that you can control the dog at all times instead of him controlling you.

Insist that the dog's inoculation record is up to date. If not, the owner must get this done before you start. If any part of your service involves taking the dog outside, he needs to be protected from rabies, worms, fleas, ticks, etc.

Your Credentials

The potential client is bound to have questions for you about your qualifications and ability to care for her dog. This is your opportunity to express your passion for dogs, your experience, and your credentials. Mention that you are insured (and bonded, if you have selected that option). Explain how you'd handle any emergency situations, including accidents or dog fights. Note any specialized training, such as pet first aid or pet CPR. You should also disclose any professional relationships you have with veterinarians if emergencies arise.

It's always good to have references. You may already have clients who have praised your reputation as a professional dog handler, or you can use the friends and family members on whom you "practiced" during the start-up phase. Other nonbusiness referrals can be useful as well. Leave a list of these supporters and their phone numbers with the potential client.

> ## First-Aid Training
>
> It's an excellent idea to learn pet first aid, including CPR. The Red Cross offers training classes specifically for the treatment of animals at many of their locations. You can also check with your local humane society or community college for pet-related first-aid classes.

Planning Your Schedule

Before making a final decision to take on the client, take your notes and evaluate how this client will work within your schedule and geographic area. This is a very important step in the process and one where many dog service providers run into trouble.

Write down the time it takes to get the potential client's house or apartment. Add in the actual pet sitting time and then the time it takes to get to your next client.

It often makes sense to do a test run during the time of day you are considering. I highly recommend this because some service providers underestimate morning traffic, school buses running in the area, or anything else that makes delays inevitable. By doing this, you'll be able to determine how many clients you can take on and which services you can provide. Ultimately, this is what drives your revenue stream in your dog sitting business.

If after the test run you are comfortable with the schedule and have a good feeling about the dog and potential client, call the dog owner and let her know. Hopefully, the client will feel the same and hire you. Now it's time to sign the agreement.

The Agreement

For every client, you must have a signed agreement that covers the specifics of your pet sitting sessions. The contract establishes a detailed understanding of the services you will

You need to figure out how each client will work in your dog sitting schedule.

provide, the frequency of the services, and your current billing rates. This is your best protection against misunderstandings later.

The agreement should list the additional charges for last-minute or emergency requests. You will work hard to make a logistical and efficient schedule of visits to clients' homes. Any unplanned "add-ons" will affect this tight schedule. When someone calls at the last minute for a weekend or additional visit, a surcharge will be applied. The agreement should state how much it will cost.

Similarly, if a client cancels a visit, she will be charged. Part of your agreement should be that you need a certain amount of notice for cancellation (usually 48 hours), or a charge of some sort will apply. You can determine what you are comfortable with, but I would suggest at least the cost of one night of services. This is a business for you, and if a client waits

Tipping

Some dog sitters include a line in the contract about tips, basically stating that gratuities are appreciated and go directly to the service provider. Many people tip for exceptional service from waitresses, paper delivery people, and the like. But you or your employees should not expect or demand tips. Some clients choose to provide an annual tip or bonus at the end of the year near the holidays.

until the last minute to cancel, you'll be unable to fill that spot. This is not a whimsical business, and your agreement should make that clear.

Your agreement should state your holiday rates. Thanksgiving, Christmas, and Easter are popular times for many dog owners to use your service above and beyond your normal routine visits. You should charge a fixed surcharge for holiday time.

Any discounts for referring your business should also be in your agreement. A client can reduce her bill by bringing in new customers to your business. You might offer a reduced rate or provide a free service, depending on the situation. Make sure to state that the offer will apply after the new client has enrolled in your pet sitting business. Referrals are the best way to expand your customer base, so it's a great incentive.

I have included a sample agreement in the Appendix: Form 11. It covers when the dog is to be fed, walked, or taken to appointments, as well as any light chores that were discussed at the interview. Note that this is not an official legal document—it's meant only as a guide. I highly recommend having an attorney review the agreement for your protection.

Agreement Review

Before you finish the initial interview with potential clients, leave a sample of your agreement so that they can review it.

Client Instructions Page

You'll need a form for the client to fill out that includes emergency numbers and instructions on caring for her dog. The form should include feeding instructions, medications the dog is taking and instructions for their use, any other special needs the dog may have, and written confirmation of any additional services upon which you have agreed. It is also wise to get information on the general time of arrival and departure—when you should arrive and how long you should stay. You could even include questions about the dog's routine, his temperament, sleeping habits, and favorite toys. It is best to put everything in writing so that there are no surprises later.

This form should be filled out at the same time as your client signs the contract but on a separate page from the contract. (For a sample, see the "Intake Application" in the Appendix: Form 4. This form can be modified for your dog sitting business.)

If you will be watching more than one dog for the same client, fill out a separate form for each dog to keep their information separate. This will ensure that there is no question of what is needed for each dog's care.

Day-to-Day Operations

Like most new adventures, there will be some wrinkles in your first weeks of operation. This might include modifying your schedule—if this happens, your client should be part of any decisions involving a change in your service.

Let's take a look at some other issues that are bound to crop up for a pet sitting business.

In-Home Visits

After you have a signed contract, it's time to get started. Ask your client all of the important questions before you perform the service:

- Is the dog allowed on any of the furniture, like the bed or the couch?
- Is he free to roam in every room, or are there any that are off-limits?
- What time does he usually go outside to eliminate?
- Does he eat before going outside?
- Are snacks allowed?
- Are there alarms that must be reset before you leave the residence?
- Where or what is the security code?

Overnight Stays

If you offer overnight stays as part of your service, you'll want to treat the client's home just as you'd want your own home treated. Lock all of the doors and windows coming and going. Tidy up after any mishaps. Reset the thermostat at the level you found it when you came in. Your client's home should be in the same shape as when she left it in your care.

Ask your client about any limitations she'd prefer to set while you are in the house. For example, certain rooms may be off-limits, the home phone should be used only in case of emergency, visitors aren't allowed, etc. You have been hired to care for the dog, and some restrictions are not only understandable but necessary.

By the way, your client has the right to have hidden surveillance cameras installed for the safety of her pet and home. So don't be surprised if you are viewed or taped while you are in your client's home.

Ask your client about any rules concerning the dog, like if he's allowed on the bed.

Multi-Dog Tip
If you will be dog sitting for more than one dog in the same household, offer a discount—say, half off your fee for the second dog.

Safety

A big consideration when it comes to your dog sitting service is the safety of both you and the dogs. Here are some tips for keeping everyone safe.

- *Never leave the dog alone or unattended.* This is essential for his safety and protection.
- When you take the dog outside, make sure that he has an identification tag on his collar with his name, address, and telephone number.
- If you are coming to a house after dark, ask that the lights be kept on outside (if they are not automatic).
- Ask your clients to let their neighbors know that you will be dog sitting so that they don't think someone is breaking in.
- Give your client your cell phone number in case she needs to get in touch with you.
- If the house has an alarm system, make sure that you have the alarm code and the alarm company's information.
- Ask for an extra key.
- Ensure that smoke detectors are working correctly in the home.

Handling House Keys

Keys are important in your pet sitting business. As you add a new client, make a tag and attach it to the house key. Never identify the client's name or address on the key tag label. Use a numbering system or some type of code to identify the residence.

Let your client know that you will make a master copy of the key and keep it in your office at all times, for emergencies. Bring the other set with you as you do your rounds. Having a key to a client's house is a big trust issue. This makes bonding and insurance even more important to your business, especially if you end up hiring employees. A bonded employee should return all keys to the office at the end of her shift as part of the check-in/check-out procedure.

Keeping your clients' keys secure is an important part of the business.

Backup

If you cannot make an appointment at the designated time, contact your client and let her know. Don't even think about skipping an appointment or coming at a much later time without any notification. This is a surefire way to lose your customers and eventually your dog sitting business.

Emergencies are inevitable, and you'll need a contingency plan in case you are unable to get to a client's house. Identify a backup person for these times. This person can fill in when you need some time off for personal reasons. However, if a substitution is ever necessary, disclose it to your client.

If you have grown your business to the point where you have several employees, it's still a good idea to have backup personnel on call should one or more employees be unable to work for a day or longer. Pay your backup people generously—you don't want to lose them, so treat them well.

Emergencies

Cultivate a professional relationship with a local veterinarian or two. That way, if an injury occurs with a dog, you'll be able to bring him to someone you know rather than flip through the yellow pages in a panic. Many owners may prefer that their dogs be taken to the family vet, but you should let your client know that this may not be possible in some emergencies.

Paperwork

To run your dog sitting business, you'll have to take care of certain paperwork. Be as organized as you possibly can in this area—it not only makes you look more professional but will make your life easy in the long run.

Billing

Keeping track of billing is important for your business. Clients should pay up front for your service. This way, you're not chasing down people for payments. If a client prefers to pay in advance for the entire month (and many will), consider giving that client a small discount.

If you decide to accept a client who will only pay after the service is provided, you must be strict. Discontinue service for anyone more than a week behind in payments—and don't forget to add this language to your contract. However, I strongly recommend that paying up front be your policy. If a client balks at this policy, inform her that you offer a money-back guarantee if the service provided did not meet expectations.

Daily Logs

Keep a daily log for your pet sitting appointments. Although you can use an electronic device to do this, such as a Blackberry, it's always good to have a hard copy. This will serve as a paper trail to record each visit. Write down your arrival and departure times. If you have employees working for you, filling out their log and handing it in at the end of the day should be a requirement. Honesty is truly the best policy for your business. There will always be some unscrupulous dog sitters who falsify their reports, but once they are inevitably discovered, it's the end of their business. For a sample of a daily log, see Appendix: Form 12.

Report Cards

In addition to tracking your time in the log, make a note of anything unusual that happened with the dog. You can do this with a "report card" that you leave at your client's home after each visit. Comment on the dog's appetite, what he ate, and

what he did. Was he lethargic? Was he unusually energetic? Always note any medications you administered. Also include any activity that happened within the home, such as utility people coming in or phone messages.

You can leave a report card even if nothing out of the ordinary happened—the dog's conduct is always of interest to your client, even if it's to report that he's been playful or relaxed. You might note if the dog played with a certain toy while you were there or did something funny. Your clients will enjoy these report cards, and they show that you have interest in their particular dog—that it's not just a business to you.

I have included a sample doggy day care report card in the Appendix: Form 7. This can be tweaked for your pet sitting visits. You can even have this form made up with a carbon copy feature so that the client gets the original and you have a copy to file.

Keeping Clients Happy

There are many extra services and personal touches you can offer your clients to keep them loyal and content. In this business, you not only have to be a dog person, but you must be a people person as well. Consider some of the following ideas.

- Take a digital camera with you to your dog sitting appointments, and snap a few photos of the dog playing or doing something cute. Print out or e-mail the photos to your client—it's a small touch that any dog owner would love.
- Periodically buy a new toy for the dog and give it to your client. Tell her that the dog loved it when you played with it together. This personal touch goes a long way with clients.
- Arrange a play date at a pet sitting appointment with a dog from another client. This

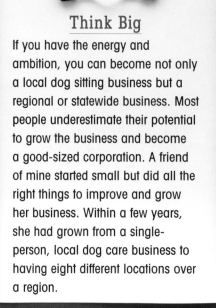

Think Big

If you have the energy and ambition, you can become not only a local dog sitting business but a regional or statewide business. Most people underestimate their potential to grow the business and become a good-sized corporation. A friend of mine started small but did all the right things to improve and grow her business. Within a few years, she had grown from a single-person, local dog care business to having eight different locations over a region.

must be cleared with both dog owners, but I have seen it work out well for everyone involved. These can also be photo opportunities.

- Don't be afraid to recommend a trip to the groomer or offer to take the dog for his routine vet visit. These services are very popular with dog owners because running these errands on weekends takes away from the client's limited personal time. Paying you to do chores like these is a reasonable alternative.
- If your client is going away on a business trip or on vacation, you might offer to care for the dog in your own home for an additional fee. Your client will feel comfortable that her dog is staying with someone she knows and trusts, and you'll add income to your business without any additional effort or travel.

Growing Your Business

It is best to start small and slowly expand your business. With experience and a good reputation, it will start to grow on its own. Your clients will talk to their friends about your excellent level of service, and soon you'll be receiving phone calls from new customers. Word of mouth is always the best and most cost-efficient form of advertising.

Spreading the Word

Even though client recommendations are your best marketing tool, there's no reason you shouldn't be proactive about expanding your customer base. Don't stop marketing your pet sitting business after the initial start-up—it's something you'll need to do continuously. Retrace your steps during the planning stage, and go back to any personal contacts you made. Return to the doggy day care center(s), the veterinary clinics, the pet supply stores, and the dog groomers, and let them know that your pet sitting business is off the ground. Take a few minutes to describe your business and tell them you're looking for clients. Then leave a handful of business cards with the manager.

Much of the marketing information in Chapter 8 is equally applicable to your dog sitting business, so take a few minutes to read that section. In addition to the ideas in that chapter, try creating a magnetic business sign with your business name, logo, phone number, and website to place on your car. This is an inexpensive investment that will catch a lot of attention as you drive around town.

Hiring Employees

As you take on new clients, you will inevitably reach a point where you can no longer service all of your customers within the arranged schedule. You now have to consider hiring assistants, and remember the golden rule: *hire slow and fire fast*. Unfortunately, too many employers do just the opposite, to the detriment of their business.

Your employees are a reflection of your business, so you want to hire the best. Get recommendations from local veterinarians, pet store owners, or even nearby kennels. You don't want to spend a lot of time interviewing just anyone who happens to love dogs—you want a select screened group of qualified applicants. Chapter 6 has detailed information about screening and interviewing potential employees. Although the hiring qualifications for a pet sitter may not be as focused as with a dog day care employee, the basic characteristics of dependability, honesty, and skillfulness at managing dogs still hold true.

One big difference between hiring a day care worker and hiring a pet sitter is that the pet sitter will have no immediate supervision. Your hired associates will be trusted with the keys to many homes and will always be unsupervised. So the most important thing to look for is hires who are trustworthy and dependable. It's wise to run your own background checks on those applying for positions within your company.

Try to hire someone who is looking to do this work permanently, not someone who just needs some quick cash. It's not fair to the dog or to your client if the dog sitter is continually changing. Be careful when interviewing, pay as well as you can, and be honest with the prospective staff member about your rules.

Business Evaluation

If you are approached by a company or individual to buy out your pet sitting business, react carefully and slowly. Remember, it took you a long time to develop and expand. You've invested thousands of hours over the years and a significant amount of money into your company. You've hired personnel and built up relationships with your clients. You must consider if you really want to retire from this rewarding venture, and if so, how much money you can make by selling it. One other factor that may play into this situation is if you have a need to sell your business. This might be predicated on unplanned life changes, illness, or relocation to another part of the country.

In any case, you've worked hard to build your business, so you should be justly compensated for your efforts. There are several business textbooks that explain how to do this, or better yet, you can take advantage of the Service Corps of Retired Executives (SCORE) once again. The counselors there can use a standard formula to determine the current monetary value of your business. As always, the free advice that goes along with this counseling can be most valuable.

If you interview, screen, and hire well, you can continue to expand your business. It's not uncommon to have pet sitting entrepreneurs move from the "front line" to simply managing the business from an administrative office. Some dog care business services get so large they become national franchises.

Preventing Burnout

The first year of running your dog sitting business will be exciting, frustrating, and rewarding as you see your business take off and expand. You'll be learning every day—about the dogs, about the owners, and about the business.

After a few years, it's possible that your days might become a little bit monotonous. This happens with any type of business, but you must always be alert and do your job— providing the dogs with the companionship, exercise, and play they require. If you find yourself losing interest, remember the dogs. They were the reason you got into this business in the first place.

Make sure that you take time off to prevent burnout.

To prevent the doldrums:

- Try modifying your schedule just a little bit to make it different. (Coordinate this with your clients, of course.)
- Continually educate yourself about dogs, including their behavior, health, and training. Read new books, magazines, and Internet sites that deal with your interests.
- Take courses for small business owners or dog professionals at your local college or community center.
- Stretch your imagination and come up with new ways to market your business.
- Take time off. Dog sitting can easily become a 12-hour-a-day, 7-day-a-week endeavor. Find a backup person and take a vacation or at least a long weekend to get away.
- If your business is growing and you've hired additional staff, consider stepping back and just managing it. This can be a welcome change to the usual routine, as it allows you to do different tasks each day to help your business at various levels. You can actually expand your business more effectively from the manager's chair.

The point is to do everything you can to make yourself refreshed and happy. This way, you can keep your charges content and loved as you perform your routine tasks.

A Day in the Life

One dog sitter I know started doing a little bit of light cleaning for one of her clients during her sessions for no charge. She thought it was a friendly gesture and a nice feature of her service. The client began asking for more and more chores without any compensation. Suddenly, the pet sitter was a house cleaner, which was not her intent at all.

Lesson of the Day: Be careful when you take on any chores while pet sitting in a client's home. Do so only if you want to and if you are fairly compensated for them.

Chapter

12

Starting a
Dog Walking Business

With dog ownership on the rise,
starting your own dog walking
business is a great option for
potential entrepreneurs.

In the past, dog walking was not necessarily a professional, organized business. Now, dog walking can be a full-time job and a great business opportunity. (Because dog walking and dog sitting have many similar aspects, you'll find some overlap from the dog sitting chapters.)

A dog walking services provides dogs the opportunity to eliminate, exercise, and get some fresh air.

What Is Dog Walking?

A dog walking service is precisely what it sounds like. The dog walker comes to the client's home, leashes the dog, and takes him for an adequate walk. The service provides the dog the opportunity to eliminate, exercise, and get some fresh air. When the walk is finished, the dog is returned to his home, unleashed, and left alone once more. Depending on the location of the business, some dog walkers walk more than one dog at a time. For instance, in cities like New York, the clients are located close together (perhaps even in the same building), and it makes good business sense to walk multiple dogs. In less urban areas, say a town in Vermont, the clients will be farther apart, and most dog walkers in these areas walk one dog at a time.

What dog walking doesn't include are most of the services provided with in-home pet sitting. There are no additional services or overnight stays. Dog walkers don't typically feed the dogs, refresh the water bowls, or tidy up the house. Because the dog walker is usually on a tight schedule and may be burdened with multiple dogs when picking up a dog or returning him to his home, there are no opportunities for her to be more than that—a dog walker.

Who Needs Dog Walkers?

The people looking for dog walkers tend to be in similar situations as those looking for pet sitters. There are dogs rejected from doggy day care for various reasons, including incompatibility with other dogs or lack of socialization. These otherwise lovely pooches just can't make it in a pack setting, but their owners still want them to have human company during the day. Also, there are owners who don't want to subject their older dogs to the stress of a new environment, and there are those who can't afford a good doggy day care center.

A professional, qualified dog walking service breaks up long, lonely days for many dogs, provides them with socialization, and showers them with care while the owner must work. It also provides peace of mind for stressed-out dog owners who feel guilty about all the time spent away from their pooch.

> ## Dogs in the City
> Dog walking services are most popular in urban areas. If you ever spend the day in New York City's east side or Boston's Back Bay section, you'll be sure to catch several dog walkers at work. Dog walking has also been booming in cities like Chicago and San Francisco over the last several decades.

Disabled Dog Owners Need Dog Walkers

A large segment of the population owns dogs but because of illness, injury, or simply aging, is unable to walk them on a routine basis. These people will be looking for a dog walking service to take their dogs out for some fresh air, play, and to eliminate. Many aspiring dog walkers overlook this special niche that could truly benefit from your service. You might inquire or leave a flyer or brochure at physical rehabilitation centers to inform patients of your services.

Are You Ready?

I've mentioned it before but it bears repeating: Do not enter into a dog care business without a real commitment. It's not fair to the dogs or your clients. Dogs thrive on routines and need to have consistency with their handlers (i.e., they want the same people caring for them and not someone different during each visit or each week).

You need to get to know each and every dog—their habits and behavior. Changing caretakers too often can be hurtful to the dog, so do not take the job lightly.

Dog Care Experience

Assuming that you have the commitment, you must have the required chemistry and experience interacting with dogs. We're not just talking about small cute pups but dogs of various breeds, sizes, and temperaments. There should be a comfort level between you and dogs. You should have some degree of technical knowledge about dogs, the various breeds, and dog behavior. You must also know when a dog is going to change behavior and possibly become aggressive and how this must be managed.

It's helpful to ask your friends and relatives if you can walk their dogs every chance you can—for free. Try to mix up the breeds and sizes to learn how to control the pack. Begin slowly walking a couple of dogs, and then increase the pack one at a time. You may pick up some potential clients, and you'll have a base of people who can recommend your service when you start out.

Don't try to walk a pack of dogs if you've never done it before—walk a few dogs at a time and gradually increase the number until you are comfortable controlling the pack.

The Shape You're In

Think about your physical ability to do this job. You will need to be in semi-good shape, and a dog walking business may be a good motivator to get into even better shape! Get a physical if there are any questions about whether you can physically handle this type of job.

All-Weather Conditions

By definition, a dog walking service takes place out of doors. You will be exposed to all types of weather, including wind, snow, heat, rain, etc. Of course, you'll protect yourself from the elements as best you can, but the dogs do have to walk. There are no days off from this service!

Start-Up

Although starting a dog walking business is not as complex as a DDC, you must still adequately plan for the start-up of your dog care business.

Feasibility Study

Chapter 2 has a detailed description of a feasibility study, but you don't need to go into quite as much detail for your dog walking business. The first part of the feasibility study is to determine if your area can support a dog walking business. Go to your town hall and ask for a list of registered dog owners. Visit pet care businesses in your area, such as veterinary offices, pet stores, and groomers, and ask if the staff thinks that there would be any interest in such a service.

You will also want to adopt the same principle regarding the geographic density of clients as a pet sitting business. You must keep your clients in close proximity, or you will lose time and money traveling from one client to another. In urban areas, some dog walkers only provide the service within a small grid of city blocks. This allows them to avoid the need for vehicular transportation or mass transportation between clients. This way, they can pick up, walk, and return the dogs efficiently.

Join a Club

Although there aren't any specific national organizations for dog walkers, consider joining the National Association of Professional Pet Sitters (NAPPS) and Pet Sitters International (PSI). They cover all types of information for pet professionals. Joining a professional organization looks good on your resume and shows clients you are serious about your business.

Competition

Just as with a pet sitting business, use the Internet and yellow pages to see what kind of competition you are up against. Look for serious businesses, not part-time or after-school dog walkers just doing it for a bit of pocket money. Also, ask around at local pet care businesses, like veterinary offices, pet supply stores, and groomers.

Call the competition and ask about their rates and services so that you will have a good idea of what you're up against.

Start-Up Costs

It is relatively inexpensive to start a dog walking service. You'll need the following:
- baggies for poop
- business cards
- cell phone
- computer (optional—you can track your clients by hand in the beginning)
- insurance/bonding premiums (see section "Insurance and Bonding")
- leashes
- pooper scooper

- portable water bowls
- reliable vehicle
- travel expenses, including gas

The leashes, water bowls, pooper scooper, and baggies can be brought with you in a backpack on your walk. Most dogs will have their own leashes or harnesses, but you should always have an extra leash with you for emergencies.

Determining Rates and Fees

Your dog walking rates will vary depending on your location. If you are in the city, you'll be able to charge more per session. Many dog walkers offer rates for 20-minute, 45-minute, and hour-long walk/play sessions. If a client has more then one dog it is a good idea to offer to walk the second dog at half price.

Think about expanding the services you offer. If your client has other animals, such as cats or rabbits, offer to feed them and clean the litter for a fee. You can also take dogs to the veterinarian or groomer. You can even offer to do the shopping for the pets. Think about services that would be helpful to your clients and save them time.

If the customer prefers more walks than your standard policy, you can charge accordingly. This is something you have to determine as you gain more experience. Also, you will find that the relationship you build with the dog owner becomes a significant factor in charging for any extra services.

Insurance and Bonding

Unfortunately, we live in a society with unscrupulous service providers and homeowners. Your dog walking business involves you coming into your client's house alone to pick up the dog. Bad things can happen, including missing or damaged items, which may or may not have been your fault. To protect yourself from potential lawsuits, you're going to need liability insurance.

You can be sued for negligence, property damage, and everything in between. Most of the times these claims have no merit, but the cost of hiring an attorney can be significant.

To protect yourself and your business, get proper insurance coverage.

To protect yourself and your business, get proper insurance coverage.

If you've hired an attorney or consultant to help you with any part of the start-up, you may want to ask her for help finding the best coverage. There are various insurance options to choose from, but I've found that Pet Sitters International (PSI) and the National Association of Professional Pet Sitters (NAPPS) are able to provide discounted rates through their insurance partners to dog walkers. Get good general liability coverage, which can protect you while you are in the client's home, your own home, or in transit. You can check their websites for estimated costs for the coverage you need.

Workman's Comp

As I mentioned in Chapter 10, it is wise to have a workman's compensation policy for you and your employees in case of bodily injury, such as a dog bite. This insurance is often mandated in most states.

Some dog walkers also choose to become legally bonded. This is usually only necessary when you have hired employees, as bonding basically protects you in case of employee theft. (If you are the only employees, there's not much chance you'll be stealing from your clients and putting your business in jeopardy!) I strongly suggest that you study the policies of the bonding organization carefully, and understand what protection you are going to have before you buy it. Like insurance policies, a variety of coverage programs are available, and both the PSI and NAPPS offer bonding. Some dog walkers choose to get bonded simply as a marketing tool, even if they don't have any employees. To many clients, saying "fully insured and bonded" sounds pretty good!

Marketing and Advertising

If you have the money, you can advertise your dog walking business in your local newspaper. However, there are many other inexpensive and effective ways to market your pet sitting business.

The Business Name

We've spoken about coming up with a catchy name for your business in prior chapters, but it bears repeating here. Use the sample word grid in Chapter 3 to help inspire you to name your dog walking service. Then check online to make certain that your choice isn't already in use. After you have selected the name (and perhaps created a logo), print business cards, flyers, letterhead stationary, and brochures with your special brand on them.

Cold-Calling

During your feasibility study, you may gain access to dog owners' phone numbers from the town hall. If so, dedicate several nights to telephone solicitations. Although cold-calling isn't terribly fun, it can be productive, and your call just might solve some dog owner's dilemma. Keep your street map by your side as you make each call. When you talk to each dog owner, tell them the purpose of your call, and ask if there is any interest in your pet sitting services. If so, make an appointment to meet the owner and the dog.

Business Cards

Your business cards are your calling cards and need to leave a good impression when you give them out. (See Chapter 8 for detailed instructions on designing your business card.) Be sure to carry them on you at all times, whether in a business or social setting. You never know who may be interested in your business, so always offer to give your card to new people you meet.

Flyers

Flyers are probably the best way to advertise your dog walking business and solicit clients. The flyer should explain the purpose of your business, the services you are offering, a bit about your experience as a dog handler (optional), and of course, your telephone number. You might consider including a discount coupon for the first visit to entice clients to call you.

- Post flyers at various pet-related businesses, such as veterinary offices, pet stores, etc.
- Visit your local hospital and ask the administration if you can post your flyers at predetermined points within the facility. Some patients may have dogs at home and family or friends unable to care for them. Although the assignment may only be for a short time, these engagements often turn into long-term business relationships.
- Retirement communities that are restricted to elderly people with no children could also be a great potential source of prospective clients. Ask at the front desk if you can leave your flyers out or on a bulletin board.
- Don't forget to pay a visit to the local dog shelter. Many of these dogs are adopted by caring and sensitive owners who can use your services. Make sure that the shelter has your flyers and business cards to hand out to adopting dog owners.

Websites

Creating a website for your dog walking business isn't a necessity, but it certainly doesn't hurt and can give the impression of a stable business. It is always best to try to develop your own website without relying on professional website developers. Creating your own site using a template is much easier than you think—there are literally hundreds of software programs to assist you in developing your site. You can then edit the text any way you want and upload your digital photos. You can make changes as you see fit without incurring the charges that come with hiring someone. This approach reduces the capital cost of hiring a webmaster and eliminates the continuous costs of maintaining the site.

If you decide to create a website, it should only have the basic essentials of your walking business and the services you provide. Don't list your fee structure on the website—if the web surfer is sincerely interested, she can call you. But remember, "www" stands for World Wide Web," so don't be surprised to get calls from people not logistically close to you and who won't turn out to be viable clients.

A website can be a good extra marketing tool, so make sure that it is printed on all of your marketing material, including business cards, letterhead, etc.

Dog walking provides a great business opportunity with very low start-up costs. Now let's take a look at what running a dog walking business is like.

A Day in the Life

One of my all-time favorite dogs I ever walked was a 60-pound (27-kg) Bulldog named Tank. I walked him faithfully three times per week for about six months. One spring morning, I picked up Tank and decided to drive him to the cranberry bogs for a good long walk instead of our usual suburban route. (As always, I made sure that I had my client's permission to take the dog in my car.) Tank seemed like he had lots of energy that particular day, so I thought he'd love the change in venue. I pulled up to the bog and he jumped out of the car ready and raring to go. About halfway through the 1.5-mile (2.4-km) trek around the bog, Tank decided that he was done walking and lay down for a nap. There was nothing I could do to entice him to finish the walk, so I had to carry him back to the car...did I mention that he weighed 60 pounds (27 kg)??

Lesson of the Day: You may want to stick close to home and follow a regular walking routine, or you might get more exercise than you anticipated.

Chapter

13

Operating Your
Dog Walking Business

Dog walking is a fairly easy and low-cost venture to
set up. Now let's lookat some of the day-to-day operating
issues. (Because dog walking and dog sitting have many
similar aspects, you'll find some overlap from the dog
sitting chapters.)

The Initial Interview

Once you have potential dog walking clients interested in your business, it's time to schedule the interview. This initial application interview is critically important, and you must be thoroughly prepared. This is not a one-way interview—you and the potential client will be interviewing each other. You need to get a feel for the chemistry between you and the client, and this is also the time to find out how the dog reacts to and interacts with you.

Don't Make Snap Decisions

The first thing you should make clear during the interview is that no contractual decisions will be made at this initial meeting. You need to give yourself the option of considering everything you learned during the interview and then politely calling back to either accept or turn down the assignment. Take your time in deciding on the clients and the dogs you'll be taking—even if the dog belongs to a relative or friend.

Services Provided

Next, discuss the number of walks per week and the length of time per walk.

Again, this is for informational purposes—you are not agreeing to do anything at this point.

You must be serious and committed to the service you offer. The motto for your business should be "underpromise and overdeliver"—so if you promise to walk the dog for a half hour, you must not take shortcuts and walk him for only 15 or 20 minutes.

The Dog

While the interview is taking place, play with the dog (in a subtle manner, if possible). You want to take him for a trial walk without the owner—dogs, like children, act differently when the parent is not around. This is the litmus test and should tell you how the relationship will work with the dog. It is paramount that

During the initial interview, ask about the dog's walking habits.

you feel comfortable and that there is good chemistry between you and the dog. You should feel that you can control the dog at all times instead of him controlling you.

Discuss items like leashes, collars, or harnesses used for walking the dog. Ask about the dog's habits while he walks— does he lunge, chew on the leash, or run after cars? Does he typically take his time before eliminating? Find out as much as you can about the individual dog. If you are walking multiple dogs, tell the owner that you'd like to take a trial walk with the rest of the pack you walk to see how he behaves while leashed with other dogs.

First Aid for Pets

Any dog care professional should know the basics of pet first aid. The Red Cross offers animal-specific pet first-aid courses, including CPR. There are also online classes available, and you can always check with your vet, as she may know of such classes in your area.

You must insist that the dog's inoculation record be up to date. If not, the owner must get this done before you start. Because your service involves taking the dog outside and into the neighborhood, he needs to be protected from rabies, worms, fleas, ticks, and other diseases. There are many ubiquitous pests that can easily be picked up from other dogs.

Your Credentials

The potential client is bound to have questions for you about your qualifications and ability to walk and care for her dog. This is your opportunity to express your passion for dogs, your experience, and your credentials. Mention that you are insured (and bonded, if you have selected that option). Explain how you'd handle any emergency situations, including accidents or dog fights. Note any specialized training, such pet first aid or pet CPR. You should also disclose any professional relationships you have with veterinarians if emergencies arise.

It's always good to have references. You may already have clients who have praised your reputation as a professional dog handler, or you can use the friends and family members on whom you "practiced" during the start-up phase. Other nonbusiness referrals can be useful as well. Leave a list of these supporters and their phone numbers with the potential client.

Planning Your Schedule

Before making a final decision to accept the client, take your notes and evaluate how this client will work within your schedule and geographic area. This is a very important step in the process and one where many dog service providers run into trouble.

If you are planning on doing single dog walks (one dog at a time), calculate your travel time (with and without traffic), plus your actual time walking the dog, and then add a bit of extra time for getting the dog situated back in the house. For instance, 15 minutes of travel time to get to your client plus a 30-minute walk is not just 45 minutes. You have to add in a extra few minutes for getting the dog in the house, filling up his water bowl, and having him settle back in before you leave. This entire walk should be calculated at a full hour.

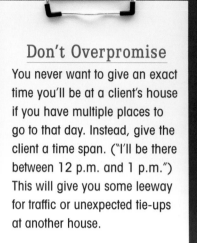

If you are taking out multiple dogs, the same time-span rules apply. If you are taking groups of dogs out, they will need to reside in close proximity. Create a "circle" of clients that makes sense, and calculate the time it will take to walk the entire group. (Remember, whichever dog you pick up first must be the first one dropped off.)

If you are comfortable with the schedule after the test run and have a good feeling about the dog and potential client, call the dog owner and let her know. Hopefully, the client will feel the same and hire you. Now it's time to sign the agreement.

The Agreement

For every client, you must have a signed agreement that covers the specifics of your dog walking sessions. The agreement establishes a detailed understanding of the services you will provide, the frequency of the services, and your current billing rates. This is your best protection against misunderstandings later.

The agreement should list the additional charges for last-minute or emergency requests. You will work hard to make a logistical and efficient schedule of walks. Any unplanned

Make sure that the terms of your dog walking arrangement are clear to your client.

"add-ons" will affect this tight schedule. When someone calls at the last minute for a change in the schedule or an additional walk, a surcharge will be applied. The agreement should state how much it will cost.

Similarly, if a client cancels a visit, she will be charged, but it's typical to allow a cancellation within a certain period (usually 24-hour notice) without a charge. Your clients need to understand that this is your livelihood, and you take it seriously.

Your agreement should state your holiday rates. You should charge a fixed surcharge for holiday time.

Any discounts for referring your business should also be in your agreement. A client can reduce her bill by bringing in new customers to your business. You might offer a reduced rate or provide a free service depending on the situation. Make sure to state that the offer will only apply after the new client has enrolled in your dog walking business. Referrals are the best way to expand your customer base, so this is a great incentive.

> **Agreement Review**
> Before you finish the initial interview with potential clients, leave a sample of your agreement so that they can review it.

For a sample agreement, see Appendix: Form 11. This can be modified to cover the services you will provide. Please note that this is not an official legal document—it's meant only as a guide. I highly recommend having an attorney review the agreement for your protection.

Client Instructions Page

You'll need a form for the client to fill out that includes emergency numbers and instructions on caring for her dog. The form should include feeding instructions, medications the dog is taking and instructions for their use, any other special needs the dog may have, and written confirmation of any additional services upon which you have agreed. Even if you are only walking the dog, it's a good idea to have all information before you take on a job. Also, give your client some idea of your general arrival and departure times.

You can even include questions about the dog's routine, temperament, sleeping habits, and favorite toys. It is best to put everything in writing so that there are no surprises later.

This form should be filled out at the same time as your client signs the agreement but on a separate page from the agreement. For a sample, see Appendix: Form 4, which can be modified for your dog walking business.

Day-to-Day Operations

Now that you know how easy it can be to set up your own dog walking business, let's discuss some of the important issues about this type of dog care.

Pickups

Before you pick up a dog, you need to know if he's a "runner" (i.e., escaper) so that you can be prepared for when that door opens. Always be on guard—when the door opens, the dog is your responsibility.

Walking Single Dogs

Although dog walking is typically not a one-on-one business, there are ways to make this work in a more suburban area. A suburban dog walker will "pick up" the dog (meaning go to the house, get him on a leash, and walk outside) and keep him in the area in which he's comfortable walking. Some owners may prefer that the dog only be let out and played with in the backyard, while others will be comfortable with you taking the dog around the neighborhood.

Walking Multiple Dogs

Most dog walkers find themselves exercising and caring for multiple dogs simultaneously. The number of dogs you can walk together will vary, depending on the size and mix of breeds. You probably don't want to walk three Mastiffs and two Silky Terriers at the same time. Experience and common sense will dictate how you schedule walking your mix of dogs, and it will really depend on their temperaments and personalities. (I had a couple of very mellow Golden Retrievers who enjoyed walking with a Bulldog and a Boston Terrier.) When I walked multiple dogs, I always tried to get the mix correct. It only takes one dog who can't tolerate walking with another dog to ruin a fine day—and perhaps even your business.

How Many Is Too Many?

Most professional dog walkers agree that walking between four and six dogs is the right amount for your pack. With four dogs, you are certainly able to focus and be alert. With six dogs, it's a bit more challenging but still doable. When I go to cities and see more than six dogs walking in a pack, I'm not only disappointed but nervous about the dogs' safety. And pedestrians are often anxious and intimidated when they see a huge pack of dogs coming at them, despite being leashed. This type of dog walker is simply trying to increase her profit while risking the safety and protection of the dogs.

As of this writing, there are few statutory regulations regarding dog walking. The city of San Francisco is drawing up legislation on the maximum number of dogs that can be

Dog Parks?

After you are comfortable with a dog's personality and know how he will react to a large number of dogs, you may want to give a dog park a try. If any of your dogs is up for that much company, it can be a great way to expend some pent-up energy. (Of course, you'll need your clients' permission.) However, I cannot stress enough: Know your dogs!

simultaneously walked, setting the upper limit to six dogs. However, writing the law is the easy part—enforcing it is the difficult part.

There will always be people who stretch the rules. Because of the explosive growth of new dog care businesses, more laws and regulations will become necessary. Hopefully, they'll separate the wheat from the chaff. The true professional dog care provider will have no problem following the laws that are in the best interest of the animal.

Safety

Another big consideration when it comes to your dog walking service is the safety of both the dogs and the walkers. Here are some tips for keeping everyone safe.

- The cardinal rule for dog walking is never leave the dogs alone or unattended, which is essential for the safety and protection of the dogs. This can prove challenging when you have four or five dogs on leashes and you have to drop one off or pick one more up to add to the pack. In this case, you will need to bring all of the dogs with you to the client's front door.
- Don't leave the dogs tied up to a utility pole or another fixed object.
- Don't ask a stranger, either adult or child, to watch the dogs while you visit a client or make a stop. You are responsible for the care and safety of the dogs the entire time they are with you.
- Make sure that each dog has an identification tag on his collar with his name, address, and telephone number.

Operating Your Dog Walking Business

You must be alert at all times when you are walking the dogs.

- Protect yourself and the dogs from inclement weather. Some owners will have rain gear available for their dogs. However, you should at least be prepared with an umbrella.
- Be alert at all times. Walking dogs can become a relaxing routine, and it's easy to start daydreaming or have your mind on other things. But there are dangers everywhere—intersections, unleashed dogs, motorcycles, cars, bicyclists, strollers, and joggers. Keep focused as you shepherd your pack of dogs through the neighborhood.
- Pick a dog walking route that is well lit to prevent accidents or unexpected mishaps. This is especially necessary during the winter, when it becomes dark earlier, and some neighborhoods become more treacherous to walk through.
- Consider carrying pepper spray or a personal body alarm as a safeguard. This can protect you and the dogs. Some of the dogs you are walking may have a high street monetary value, and dog thieves lurk in every part of the country.
- Clip a small water spray bottle to your belt in case of dog fights (amongst the pack or with loose animals).
- Always carry your cell phone with you while walking the dogs. As your business grows and you hire assistants, they too must carry a cell phone with them during the walking engagements.
- If you've hired employees, train them to check in and out with you each day. You'll have developed regular routes for your schedule, so you'll know where everyone should be at various times during the day. Stress the importance of this routine for everyone's safety.

Planning Your Route: It's all About the Poop

As part of your planning, you must determine where you can take the dogs to defecate and urinate. This can be a small grassy area, a park, or any other site that is conducive to dogs eliminating. However, make sure that it's not private property.

After the dogs relieve themselves, you must quickly and efficiently pick up the poop. Have a plastic poop bag at your fingertips and pick up all the waste. You may need to temporarily transfer that bag into a larger bag while you're waiting for any other dogs to do their thing.

When the mission's accomplished, seal the large bag and dispose of it in a proper trash or refuse container. Find out if there are any town or county restrictions on excrement disposal. Most areas allow disposal in public trash receptacles, but some towns have restrictions on how this is done.

Unfortunately, there are many dog owners who don't participate in the civil courtesy of scooping poop. But as a professional dog care provider, you must always do this task. Hopefully, others will follow by example.

Take note of each dog's excrement. It doesn't sound appealing, but this is an important health check. If you notice any abnormality, report it to the dog owner on the "report card" (see section below) or a follow-up phone call. Our best friends can't speak to us, so we have to help them whenever we can—your clients will appreciate it.

Although it's not the most pleasant aspect of the job, you must dispose of waste properly on your walks.

Drop-Offs

After the allotted time for the walk is over, you'll bring each dog back to his house. You must make sure that he is safely returned into his home environment. House keys should always be returned to the appropriate spot unless the owner has arranged otherwise. If you have staff walking the dogs, part of the standard routine should be that the keys are dropped back at your office daily. This reassures your client that you are the only one responsible for the house keys, and they are not floating around town somewhere.

Handling House Keys

Keys are important in your dog walking business. As you add a new client, make a tag and attach it to the house key. Never identify the client's name or address on the key tag label. Use a numbering system or some type of code to identify the residence.

Let your client know that you will make a master copy of the key and keep it in your office at all times, for emergencies. Bring the other set with you as you do your rounds. Having a key to a client's house is a big trust issue. This makes bonding and insurance even more important to your business, especially if you end up hiring employees.

Backup

If you cannot make an appointment at the designated time, contact your client and let her know. Don't even think about skipping an appointment or coming at a much later time without any notification. This is a surefire way to lose your customers and eventually your business.

Emergencies are inevitable, and you'll need a contingency plan in case you are unable to get to a client's house. Identify a backup person for these times. This person can fill in when you need some time off for personal reasons. However, if a substitution is ever necessary, you need to disclose it to your client.

If you have grown your business to the point where you have several employees, it's still a good idea to have backup personnel on call should one or more employees be unable to work for a day or longer. Pay your backup people generously—you don't want to lose them, so treat them well.

Emergencies

Cultivate a professional relationship with a local veterinarian or two. That way, if an injury occurs with a dog, you'll be able to bring him to someone you know rather than flip through the yellow pages in a panic. Many owners may prefer that their dogs be taken to the family vet, but you should let your client know that this may not be possible in some emergencies.

Paperwork

To run your dog walking business, you'll have to take care of certain paperwork. Be as organized as you possibly can in this area—it not only makes you look more professional but will make your life easy in the long run.

Billing

Keeping track of billing is important for your business. Clients should pay up front for your service. This way, you're not chasing down people for payments. If a client prefers to pay in advance for the entire month (and many will), consider giving that client a small discount.

If you decide to accept a client who will only pay after the service is provided, you must be strict. Discontinue service for anyone more than a week behind in payments—and don't forget to add this language to your contract. However, I strongly recommend that paying up front be your policy. If a client balks at this policy, inform her that you offer a money-back guarantee if the service provided did not meet expectations.

Daily Logs

Keep a daily log for your dog walking appointments. You can do this electronically, but keep it updated and print out hard copies. This will serve as a paper trail to record each visit. At

Keep a daily log for your dog walking appointments.

the very least, record the time you arrive at the house to take the dog out for his walk and the time you bring him back to his house or apartment. If you have employees working for you, filling out their log and handing it in at the end of the day should be a requirement. See Appendix: Form 12 for sample daily log.

Report Cards

In addition to tracking your time in the log, make note of anything unusual that happened with the dog. You can do this with a "report card" that you leave at your client's home after each visit. Comment on anything unusual. If you noticed a change in the dog's excrement, for example, report it. Any changes in the dog's behavior should also be noted.

You can leave a report card even if nothing out of the ordinary happened—the dog's conduct is always of interest to your client, even if it's to report that he loved the new route you've been walking or made a new buddy on his walk. Your clients will enjoy these report cards, and it shows that you have an interest in their particular dog—that it's not just a business to you.

I have included a sample doggy day care report card in the Appendix: Form 7. This can be adjusted for your dog walking business. You can even have this form made up with a carbon copy feature so that the client gets the original and you have a copy to file.

Keeping Clients Happy

You can offer your clients many extra services and personal touches to keep them loyal and content. In this business, you not only have to be a dog person, but you must be a people person as well. Consider some of the following ideas.

* Take a digital camera with you to your dog walking appointments and snap a few photos of the dog playing or doing something cute. Print out or e-mail the photos to your client—it's a small touch that any dog owner will love.
* Periodically buy new treats for the dog and give them to your client. This personal touch will go a long way.
* Don't be afraid to recommend a trip to the groomer or offer to take the dog for his routine vet visit. These services are very popular with dog owners because running these errands on weekends takes away from the client's limited personal time. Paying you to do chores like these is a reasonable alternative.
* If your client is going away on a business trip or on vacation, you might offer to care for the dog in your own home for an additional fee. Your client will feel comfortable that her dog is staying with someone she knows and trusts, and you'll add income to your business without any additional effort or travel. Dog walkers can easily turn their service into a pet sitting business and offer anything that a pet sitter would offer.

Growing Your Business

It is best to start small and slowly expand your business. With experience and a good reputation, it can grow on its own. Your clients will talk to their friends about your excellent level of service, and soon you'll be receiving phone calls from new customers. Word of mouth is always the best and most cost-efficient form of advertising.

Spreading the Word

Even though client recommendations are your best marketing tool, there's no reason you shouldn't be proactive about expanding your customer base. Don't stop marketing your dog walking business after the initial start-up—it's something you'll need to do continuously. Retrace your steps during the planning stage, and go back to any personal contacts you made. Return to the doggy day care center(s), the veterinary clinics, the pet supply stores, and the dog groomers, and let them know that your dog walking business is off the ground.

A tee shirt with your logo on it is a great way to spread the word about your business.

Take a few minutes to describe your business and tell them you're looking for clients. Then leave a handful of business cards with the manager.

Much of the marketing information in Chapter 8 is equally applicable to your dog walking business, so take a few minutes to read that section. In addition to the ideas in that chapter, try creating a magnetic business sign with your business name, logo, phone number, and website to place on your car. This is an inexpensive investment that will catch a lot of attention as you drive around town.

I have seen T-shirts, sweatshirts, and even rain ponchos made up with a dog walker's business information printed on them. These items get seen as you march your pack of dogs around and may catch a lot of new customers.

Hiring Employees

As you take on new clients, you will inevitably reach a point where you can no longer service all of your customers within the arranged schedule. You now have to consider hiring assistants, and remember the golden rule: *hire slow and fire fast*. Unfortunately, too many employers do just the opposite, to the detriment of their business.

Your employees are a reflection of your business, so you want to hire the best. Get recommendations from local veterinarians, pet store owners, or even nearby kennels. You don't want to spend a lot of time interviewing just anyone who happens to love dogs—you want a select screened group of qualified applicants. Chapter 6 has detailed information about screening and interviewing potential employees. Although the hiring qualifications for a dog walker may not be as focused as with a dog day care employee, the basic characteristics of dependability, honesty, and skillfulness at managing dogs still hold true.

Dog walkers should be skilled at managing dogs.

Make sure that you discuss the amount of exercise the job entails. Be completely honest as to what is required—that includes lifting, walking, and the strength to hold the dogs when they pull.

One big difference between hiring a day care worker and hiring a dog walker is that the dog walker will have no immediate supervision. Your hired associates will be trusted with the keys to many homes and will always be unsupervised. You need to look for trustworthy and dependable people to hire. It's wise to run your own background checks on those applying for positions within your company.

Try to hire someone who is looking to do this work permanently and not someone

Alter your walking route a little bit for a fun diversion for both you and the dog.

who just needs some quick cash. Be careful when interviewing, pay as well as you can, and be honest with the prospective staff member about your rules.

If you interview, screen, and hire well, you can continue to expand your business. It's not uncommon to have dog walking entrepreneurs move from the "front line" to simply managing the business from an administrative office. Some dog care business services get so large they become national franchises.

Preventing Burnout

The first year of running your dog walking business will be exciting, frustrating, and rewarding as you see your business take off and expand. You'll be learning every day—about the dogs, about the owners, and about the business.

After a few years, it's possible that your days might become a little bit monotonous. This happens with any type of business, but you must always be alert and do your job, providing the dogs with the companionship, exercise, and play they require. If you find yourself losing interest, remember the dogs. They were the reason you got into this business in the first place.

To prevent the doldrums:

- Try modifying your schedule just a little bit to make it different. (Coordinate this with your clients, of course.)
- Alter your walking route for a little diversion for both you and the dogs.
- Continually educate yourself about dogs, including their behavior, health, and training. Read new books, magazines, and Internet sites that deal with your interests.
- Take courses for small business owners or dog professionals at your local college or community center.
- Stretch your imagination and come up with new ways to market your business.
- Take time off. Dog walking is physically demanding and can become a seven-day-a-week endeavor. Find a backup person and take a vacation or at least a long weekend to get away.
- If your business is growing and you've hired additional staff, consider stepping back and just managing it. This can be a welcome change to the usual routine, as it allows you to do different tasks each day to help your business at various levels. You can actually expand your business more effectively from the manager's chair.

The point is to do everything you can to make yourself refreshed and happy. This way, you can keep your charges content and loved as you perform your routine tasks.

Growing your dog walking business has no limitations. If you do it right and create a reputable business, hire the right people, and are selective about adding clients, you will have happy employees, happy dog owners, and happy dogs.

A Day in the Life

I know a woman in the Boston area who built up a lucrative and reputable dog walking business. After several years, she decided that she wanted to change careers, so she offered to simply sell her client list. The response was overwhelming, and she managed to get $25,000 for her list.

Lesson of the Day: Spending years developing a solid client base through word of mouth and other marketing avenues is worth all the hard work!

Chapter

14

Dog Camps

Up to this point we have covered in some considerable degree of detail the common contemporary dog care businesses: doggy day care centers, dog sitting businesses, and dog walking services.

There is one more business that is burgeoning across the country that you may want to consider—dog camps. This unique type of dog care business has grown tremendously in the past ten years and is continuing to gain attention. Unfortunately, the necessary diligence and detail of the dog camp business require more space than we have in this book, but this chapter will highlight some of the issues involved with the enterprise.

What Are Dog Camps?

About 15 years ago, vacation places for dogs and their owners began to pop up. These spots filled the needs of dog owners who weren't happy entrusting their dog to a pet sitter or day care facility while away on vacation. These people didn't want to be separated at all from their dogs during vacation—they wanted to spend their vacation *with* their dog. Thus, the genesis of the dog camp business was born.

Currently, there are a wide variety of dog camps, but basically they are facilities for dogs and their owners to "get away from it all" and participate in recreational activities together. Some camps offer weekly stays, while others are weekend-only operations. Dog and owner sleep in the same unit (usually a cabin), so they are together overnight. During the day, a variety of activities are available, which can include hiking through the woods, swimming, dog dancing, training, and behavior modification. Usually, activities without the dog are also available, such as crafts, viewing training videos, and seminars. Contests of all stripes, including costume contests, parades, dog tricks, and show competitions, often round out the program. Dog camps have their own food services and dining facilities, so owners and dogs need not leave the campgrounds to eat. And there is plenty of free time for the owner and dog to sightsee or just spend quiet time together away from it all.

Some dog camps offer a chance to go camping with your dog.

Where Are Dog Camps Located?

Dog camps are almost always located in a rural area, which creates a pleasant change of venue for the city dweller and suburbanite alike. Both the dog and owner get away from traffic, stress, and overcrowding and learn to relax in a pastoral setting far away from the crowds.

The campsites are large— it's not unusual to find dog camps located on anywhere from 10 to 100 acres of land or more. In addition to the space, they usually include lakes, walking paths, cabins, outhouses and showers, common rooms for seminars, indoor and outdoor dining facilities, and plenty of areas earmarked for training and recreational sports. If you're considering developing and operating a dog camp as your business, land acquisition is a critical aspect of the project. And as the cost of land escalates—even in the most remote areas—it will be one of the most expensive aspects of capitalizing the business.

Starting a Dog Camp

Before you embark on this business, get thoroughly informed. Start surfing the Internet—you may be surprised how many dog camps already exist—and you can find out a lot about this unique service and its growing popularity. Most of the comprehensive websites offer a description of the environment, programs available, weekend/weekly rates, names of the employees and professional staff, and policies for attending the camp.

Developing a dog camp business is extremely complex—more so than any of the other three services we've discussed, including doggy day cares. The planning steps we discussed in Part I, including the feasibility study, business plan, and marketing process, are still critical, but there are additional factors that make this type of business venture more difficult.

If You Build It. . .

There's a great expression from the classic film *Field of Dreams*: "If you build it, they will come." This adage holds very true for the dog camp business. Often a dog camp owner sets up her campground facilities and ends up turning away prospective enrollees because of the overwhelming demand for the service. Yes, build it and they will come!

Location

For one, will people be willing to spend an entire week in your geographical region of the country? Areas with year-round comfortable weather conditions are usually better than places that have cold, harsh winters or even humid, hot summers. Still, there are some dog camps that are only open for part of the year. It's up to you to thoroughly research the location as a possible vacation spot.

Start-Up Costs

Obviously, the financial capital involved with this dog care service dwarfs what is required for doggy day care or dog sitting and walking. As I mentioned, the land and its infrastructure are very costly, but you may be surprised to learn that this may not necessarily be your most expensive financial line item. Instead, it's the staff.

One of the differences between dog camps and other dog care businesses is the staff. If you look at brochures and websites for dog camps, you'll find a list of professionally qualified staff support, including trainers, veterinarians, groomers, behaviorists, competition judges, and others. These professionals don't come cheaply, so during your planning process, you must estimate the investment to hire qualified personnel.

The good news is that many of the professionals you hire don't have to be on your payroll from week to week. Some will opt to spend just a few weeks each year at your camp and then return to their day jobs. However, there is pressure to recruit favorably so that you have the best staff on site for most of your business year.

Liability Issues

Because you are providing lodging, food, and recreational services for both dogs and their owners, liability issues are high, which will make your insurance rates high. And because of the liability issues, you must hire an attorney with experience in these types of businesses to get the best counsel. This legal expertise is particularly important when drafting the contracts for staying at the dog camp, which will be your main protection against litigation.

Experience

Ideally, you should have experience before opening up a dog camp. Strongly consider working at one for an extended period—it will become your de facto internship. If you do get a hired position at a dog camp, try to participate in (or at least learn about) every aspect of the environment and the business. This may take some time, probably more than a year, but this experience will pay benefits when you start your own dog camp. By then you'll have learned what works well and what doesn't at these types of facilities and saved yourself a pretty big learning curve. Be up-front with the dog camp owner and tell her that you want to learn as much as possible so that you can start your own operation, but assure her that it's in a distant location.

It also wouldn't hurt for you and your dog to enroll at a dog camp that looks interesting or successful for a week. And of course, it is always wise to interview dog owners who have attended dog camps and get their perspective.

Operating a Dog Camp

Operating a dog camp is just as complex as starting one. Some of the issues in this section should give you a taste of what running one entails.

Your Role

While dog camp owners must have the same commitment and passion for dogs as other dog care business owners, they are often not as hands on. If you decide to go ahead with the business, you'll have to accept that you'll be managing and coordinating rather than performing services directly. In addition to solving problems and emergencies that inevitably arise each day, you'll be scheduling future enrollees, marketing, and performing publicity engagements.

As a dog camp owner, you will be everything: manager, social director, problem solver, marketer, and whatever else comes along from day to day. Understand this before you embark on this adventure. It takes a certain type of person to do all of these things and to do them well.

> Your dog camp should offer a variety of programs for both the dog and owner.

Programs

Your dog camp should offer a variety of programs for both the dog and owner. Your clients will want the choice of participating in activities like swimming, hunting, flyball, training, dancing, or socialization programs. And there must be courses just for the dog owner, such as crafting dog collars or leashes, which your clients may or may not want to do. This is where the program scheduling challenge comes into play. You'll have to find out long before the clients arrive what programs they are going to subscribe to so that you can plan and coordinate all of the programs and personnel required. This is why your dog camp brochure and website must be professionally done with a list of all of the camp offerings. It will be the best way of scheduling the programs.

Honesty Is the Best Policy

As I've made clear throughout this book, you can't just be a dog lover to make your business successful—you need to be a people person as well. Coming to your dog camp will be the dog owner's *vacation*—your client will be paying for this stay at your camp. You must be totally forthright about the campsite, its environment, and its infrastructure. If the cabins are not insulated or if they don't have television or indoor plumbing, spell this out on your website and in any marketing materials. Many dog owners get so focused on the idea of spending a week with their dog that they forget about sleeping on industrial-grade beds or taking an outdoor shower. It's also prudent to disclose uncontrollable factors in the brochure (and especially in the contract), such as bad weather, mosquitoes, other dog camp enrollees, etc.

Keeping Clients Happy

Here are some ideas to keep your clients happy. Hopefully, they will help you get some repeat business!

- Take frequent photos/videos of the owners and their dogs during the stay, and e-mail them after they have left. This will remind your clients of the enjoyable time spent at your dog camp and encourage them to return.
- Mail birthday and holiday cards to both the dogs and their owners. This raises your business's visibility and will improve your clients' perception of your camp. Send Out Cards makes this easy and fun.
- Take the opportunity to introduce the dog owners to one another while they are staying at your camp. This makes the owners feel comfortable, and you are helping make some lasting friendships.

Dog Camp Business Potential

Like the other dog care businesses we've discussed, the potential growth of dog camps is unlimited. Some dog camps prefer to be small, limiting their enrollment to around 40 or

50 dogs and their owners each week. But many dog camps can accommodate up to 250 dogs a week. Keep in mind that this volume is a good but challenging thing. It means that you must have enough qualified, professional staff to keep the dogs and owners busy, entertained, and educated during most of the weekly stay. It also means that the number of issues, complaints, and emergencies will be higher.

On the other hand, the potential gross revenue stream is higher. Rates for dog camps vary throughout the United States and are always dependent on certain factors, including the number of dogs per owner, the number of specialized programs, and discounts given for multiple dogs or repeat attendees. In addition to the weekly attendance fees, many camps sell dog-related products for health, play, fashion, and safety. These retail products can become a lucrative cost center for the dog camp and a significant value added to the bottom line.

It's easy to see the potential for this business, but like most operations, the revenue potential is high because the capital investment and associated risks are also quite high.

I can personally see the popularity of dog camps continuing to escalate over the next decade or so. They really are a unique and useful solution to the dog care problem. But if dog camps aren't for you, keep in mind that when camp is over, the dog owner must return to a 9-to-5 work routine, still wanting the best for her pet. So the doggy day care center, dog sitting business, and dog walking service are still viable opportunities for you to live your dream!

A Day in the Life

One particularly hot August day, we set up two kiddie pools for our ten "campers" to swim in and cool off. After spending a good part of the morning outside, it was time for them to come in and find their favorite spot to take their mid-morning nap. Giselle, a miniature Dachshund, was the pack leader of the group. (That's right—don't always assume that a big dog is always the top dog.) When all of the dogs came barreling in, Giselle decided to get a drink from the water tub that was set up on the ground. She apparently wasn't quite done swimming and decided that the best place for her nap was in the water tub. Whenever another dog approached, Giselle would jump out of the tub and chase him off. You can imagine what that area looked like after a couple of minutes—the flood waters had risen!

Lesson of the Day: Make sure that all of your water stations are raised off the ground, or you'll have a mess on your hands!

Afterword

We've covered a lot of ground on starting and running your own dog care businesses. I've shared my experiences with you so that costly mistakes can be avoided. Hopefully, after reading this book, you will follow your dream of working with dogs, make a comfortable living, and become a successful entrepreneur. And while this book is primarily about you and the many business opportunities in dog care, this book is ultimately about the dogs.

Dogs are "man's best friend" for a reason. We should always show them our unconditional appreciation for all of the subtle things they contribute to our lives.

I want to help you avoid costly pitfalls when embarking on a dog care business, but I also want you to develop the best and most humane business possible to ensure that our pets are always treated well. As I noted throughout the book, the safety and well-being of the dog is always paramount.

Dogs need caretakers. If you embark on a dog care career, you'll be extending sensitive and sensible dog care when the owner cannot do so. Dogs should never be used or exploited to make a quick paycheck by anyone. Pet care facilities are popping up everywhere these days, but only the strong, the professionally sensitive, and the well-planned facilities will survive.

As you know by now, owning a pet care business is hard work but the rewards are endless. If you do decide to open your own dog care business, don't take it lightly. Be proactive about sponsoring or supporting legislation that protects dogs from abuse and establishes criteria for operating dog care businesses. Help enforce regulations and laws so that the business of dog care both now and in the future will always be a professionally run organization.

The dogs' safety and happiness should always be your top priority in this business, and the success will follow naturally. When this is done, you will be part of a wide network of successful, sensitive, dog-loving entrepreneurs. Good luck!

Millions of pets lose their lives in animal shelters each year due to overpopulation. Visit your local shelter and adopt a dog today—they make the best pets because they know that you saved them!

Appendix A: Sample Business Forms

These sample forms can be modified to fit whichever dog care business you plan to start, including day care, dog sitting, dog walking, and dog camp. These forms are for example only and should be expanded on to suit your individual needs. These forms should not be used as legal documents without a review by your attorney.

Form 1

Market Research Survey

Name:_____ Date:_____

Address: _____

City: _____ State:_____ Zip:_____

How many dogs do you have? _____

What are their ages? _____ Breed _____

Would it be beneficial to have a doggy day care in your area?

What hours of operation would be helpful to you?

Would you use the day care's cageless boarding services?

Would grooming services be of interest?

Would you be interested in training classes?

Do you have friends or neighbors who would also find this service useful?

Would you have a need for your dog to be picked up and dropped off?

Would you like the option to have us bring your dog to the vet while you are at work?

Would it be helpful for a vet to come to the premises for yearly shots, etc.?

Would you like to see products for sale, like toys, food, collars, etc.?

How important (on a scale of 1 to 10) would it be to have all of these services in one building?

Hours of Operation and Rates

Hours of Operation*

Monday Friday: 7:00 am 6:00 p.m.
Saturday & Sunday: 8:00 a.m. 5:00 p.m.

Rates**

Payment for day care services must be paid in advance of service.

Daily Rates

Half-Day Rates (in by 8:00 a.m., out by 12:00 p.m.): $15.00
Full-Day Rates: $24.00

Punch Card Rates

10-Day Pass $216.00 (1 day free)
20-Day Pass $432 (2 days free)
30-Day Pass $600 (5 days free)

(Note: Punch cards expire six months from date of purchase.)

Monthly Club Memberships

Limited: $360 (Monday Friday $18/day)
Unlimited: $420 ($15 per day)

(Note: payment due on the first day of each month)

Boarding Rates

$35/night

Boarding Rates w/Monthly Packages

Limited: $25/night + Free Bath
Unlimited: $20/night + Free Bath

Grooming

Bath (Small Dog): $25 - $35
Bath (Large Dog): $35 - $45
Medicated Bath: add $15
Nail Trims: $10.00
Anal Glands: $12.00
Massage: $50
Clips: $25 $75

For your convenience, we can keep your credit card on file for automatic billing.

*For example only. Hours will vary depending on your business needs.

**For example only. Rates will vary depending on your lcaton

Form 3

Application for Employment

Position of Interest
- ☐ Full-Time Day Care Attendant
- ☐ Part-Time Day Care Attendant
- ☐ Full-Time Groomer
- ☐ Part-Time Groomer
- ☐ Front Office
- ☐ Cleaner

Personal Information

Name _____

Address _____

City _____ State _____ Zip _____

Home Phone _____ Cell Phone _____

Social Security Number _____

How did you hear about us? _____

Referred by _____

Experience

Employer _____

Address _____ City _____ State _____

Supervisor _____ Phone Number _____

Can We Contact? ____ Yes _____ No

Position _____

Reason for Leaving _____

Dates Worked _____ to _____

Employer #2 _____

Address _____ City _____ State _____

Supervisor _____ Phone number _____

Can We Contact? Yes _____ No_____

Position _____

Reason for Leaving _____

Dates Worked _____ to _____

Signature of Applicant _____ Date _____

Intake Application

Client's Information

Name _____ Date _____

Address _____

City _____State_____ Zip _____

Phone Number _____ Cell Phone _____

Work Address_____Phone _____

Email Address _____

Emergency Contact Name _____ Phone _____

Dog's Information

Dog's Name _____ Breed _____

M/F _____ Age _____Birthday_____ Color _____

Spayed ☐   Neutered ☐

Veterinarian's Name_____ Phone _____

We must also have a hard copy of vaccination records from your vet for our records!

Rabies_____ Distemper _____ Bordetella_____Fecal Test _____

Heartworm Preventive_____Flea & Tick _____

Health Problems (please explain) _____

Is your dog currently on any medications? If so, which ones? _____

Dog's Behavior

Has your dog ever attended day care before?   Y ☐   N ☐

Has your dog been socialized? _____ Please explain_____

Is your dog aggressive?	Y ☐	N ☐	with large dogs?	Y ☐	N ☐
with food?	Y ☐	N ☐	with small dogs?	Y ☐	N ☐
with toys?	Y ☐	N ☐	with people?	Y ☐	N ☐

Please note any of your dog's habits that we should know about:_____

_____

Howw did you hear about us? _____

Form 5

Day Care & Boarding Requirements

Please read the items below and sign, indicating that you understand these requirements.

- All dogs must be on leash when entering or leaving the building.

- All dogs must be current in all required vaccinations.

- All dogs must wear a flat collar with identification tag attached

- No training collars, prong collars, or harnesses allowed.

- Client must label all bedding and blankets for boarding stays; we cannot guarantee that they will be returned in same condition

- No rawhides or toys will be allowed in the crate during their stay.

- We reserve the right to discharge your dog if it is necessary to protect the other dogs or staff members.

- We recommend that you bring your own food in during your dog's stay to prevent stomach upsets. If you choose to use our house food, there will be an additional charge.

- Holiday day care and boarding will be priced accordingly.

- Reservations required for day care and boarding. If you need to cancel your stay, please give us 24 hours' notice or an additional charge will be incurred.

- If any veterinary services are needed during your dog's stay, you will be 100% responsible for the costs and fees associated with it.

- All dogs must be checked in by 10:00 a.m.

- Boarding dogs can be dropped off by noon on the day of stay and must be picked up by noon on the day of pickup. If picked up after noon, a day care charge will be incurred.

- All dog over the age of seven months must be spayed or neutered, or they will not be accepted.

Signature _____ Date _____

Day Care Attendant:_____

Client Agreement (DDC)

Please read the items below and sign, indicating that you understand these requirements.

- I understand that I am responsible for any and all services rendered at _____

  Name of Business

- If collection proceedings are necessary, I will be responsible for any and all attorney fees incurred.

- A handling fee of $25* will be applied on any returned checks.

- I will not hold _____ responsible for any damage or loss incurred by participating in said doggy day care program.

- It is my responsibility to make sure that my dog is properly vaccinated. I also understand that even though all dogs are properly vaccinated in the facility, a medical situation could arise due to the communal group of dogs. I will be responsible for all and any medical costs.

- I understand that even though all pets are closely monitored, there is risk involved, including scrapes and cuts, which are commonplace due to the nature of dog play. More serious injuries cannot be predicted. I give permission for [name of business] employees or a veterinarian to administer treatment to my dog. I understand that an employee from [name of business] will do his or her best to contact me first before treatment.

- I understand the center's hours of operation and understand that additional fees are applied to late pickups.

- 48-hour cancellation notice required or a fee will be incurred.

Signature _____ Date _____

Manger: _____

*For example only.

Report Card

Dear Mom & Dad,

I just wanted to give you an update of what my stay was like at!

_____
Name of Business

I missed you while you were gone but I had so much fun with all of my friends, especially _____ ; he/she
was my favorite play buddy!   *Name of Playmate*

Here is my Report Card:

Breed:

Dog's Name:

Age: Dates of Stay:

Stool
None ☐ Firm ☐ Diarrhea ☐ Soft ☐ Bloody ☐ Worms ☐

Urine
None ☐ Normal ☐ Bloody ☐ Excessive ☐

Energy Level
Very excited ☐ Kind of lazy ☐ Very happy ☐ Cuddly ☐

Interaction with my friends
They all loved me ☐ Temperamental ☐
Just wanted to have fun ☐ Cranky ☐

Appetite
None ☐ Fierce ☐ Picky ☐ None

Day Care Staff Comments: _____
_____
_____

My favorite part of my stay was: _____
_____
_____

Thanks for bringing me to _____ Doggy Day Care.
Name of Business

Please bring me back soon!
Love,

Buddy 🐾

Incident Report

Date of Incident _____ Time _____

Dog's Name _____ Owner's Name_____

Please describe the incident: _____

_____

_____

_____

Injuries sustained: _____

_____

_____

Medical attention administered: _____

Client notified   Y ☐   N ☐
Follow-up required?   Y ☐   N ☐

Day Care Attendant on Duty: _____

Signature:_____

Daily Check-In Tracking Form

Date	Dog's Name	Day Care/ Boarding	Club Y/N	Paid Y/N	Lunch Y/N	Bath Y/N

Bed & Breakfast Reservation Form

Dog's Name _____

Owner's Name _____ Phone # _____

Date of Check-In _____ Drop-Off Time _____

Date of Checkout_____ Pickup Time _____

Bath? _____ Nail Trim?_____ Clip? _____

Eating Schedule: A.M. _____ Noon_____P.M. _____ Wet/Dry?_____

Medications _____

Emergency Contact Name _____

Emergency Contact Number _____

Vet's Name _____Phone Number _____

Items checked in _____

Check-In Attendant _____

Client Agreement (Dog Sitting/Walking)

This agreement is made between _____ and
Client

_____ retaining Pet Sitter for service agreed as follows.
Pet Sitter

Client agrees to the following services (please initial):

(   ) Feeding _____ times a day

(   ) Walking _____ times a day for _____(hours) in length

(   ) Transporting to vet appointment

(   ) Transporting to and from grooming appointment

(   ) Cleaning cat litter box (or other animal)

(   ) Watering plants

(   ) Gathering mail and newspapers

(   ) Administering pet medication

(   ) Completing daily Report Card

I _____will provide the following:
Client

☐ Spare house keys (will be returned or left on final visit)
☐ Alarm code
☐ Garage door opener (if applicable)
☐ Food and treats for dog and leashes and collars unless otherwise noted
☐ Contact information in case of emergency
☐ Vet contact information
☐ Signed "Permission to Treat" form

Client understands that the following payment options are cash, check, money order, or major credit card. Balance due within ten days of last visit. There will be a \$_____ fee on all returned checks. A fee will be incurred for any cancellations without 24 hours' notice.

Client understands that Pet Sitter will carry liability insurance.

Holiday Rates: A \$_____ additional charge will incur for all holidays.

Client:_____ Date: _____

Daily Log

Date	Dog's Name	Arrival Time	Departure Time	Mileage	Food Y/N	Paid Y/N

Appendix B: First-Aid Kit

A first-aid kit can save a dog's life, and it's an essential item to keep on hand at a doggy cay care center. You can also put a kit together and keep it in your car if you are dog sitting or walking.

Basic items should include:

✓ **Activated charcoal:** For poisonings.

✓ **Antihistamine tablets:** For insect stings and allergic reactions.

✓ **Betadine or Nolvasan:** For cleaning open wounds.

✓ **Blunt-nosed scissors:** To cut tape and clip hair.

✓ **Canine rectal thermometer:** For taking dog's temperature.

✓ **Cortisone ointment:** Topical anti-inflammatory.

✓ **Cotton balls and swabs:** Various uses, such as cleaning wounds.

✓ **Eyedropper or dosage syringe:** To apply medication.

✓ **Eyewash:** To irrigate eyes.

✓ **First-aid cream:** To soothe and protect wounds.

✓ **Gloves:** Two pairs one set of thin plastic gloves to prevent contamination and heavy gloves if you fear being bitten.

✓ **Hand towel:** Cleaning up, drying hands, etc.

✓ **Hydrogen peroxide (3 percent):** Various uses, such as for inducing vomiting.

✓ **Ipecac or hydrogen peroxide:** To induce vomiting.

✓ **Kaolin and pectin:** To help diarrhea.

✓ **Magnifying glass:** To locate tiny objects.

✓ **Muzzle:** Even the nicest dog can snap if he's in pain. Have a muzzle on hand for safety.

✓ **Nail clippers:** In case of an accident to the nail bed.

✓ **Nonstick adhesive tape:** For taping bandages.

✓ **Nonstinging antiseptic spray or swabs:** For cleaning wounds.

✓ **Petroleum jelly:** To accompany the rectal thermometer; also for constipation.

✓ **Poison Control phone number:** (888)-426-4435

✓ **Saline solution:** Various uses, such as irrigating wounds.

✓ **Stretch bandage:** For wounds.

✓ **Styptic pencil:** To stop minor bleeding.

✓ **Tweezers or hemostat:** To pull out splinters and other foreign objects.

✓ **Two rolls of gauze bandages:** For wrapping wounds.

✓ **Vet's emergency phone number**

Appendix C: Websites

Copyright and Trademark Searches

Legalzoom.com
www.legalzoom.com

MyCorporation
www.mycorporation.intuit.com

The Trademark Directory
www.trademark.org

United States Copyright Office
www.copyright.gov

Domain Name Search

1&1
www.1and1.com

Go Daddy.com
www.godaddy.com

Register.com
www.register.com

First Aid

ASPCA National Animal Poison Control Center
www.aspca.org/pet-care/poison-control/
Phone: (888) 426-4435

Red Cross
www.redcross.org/services/hss/courses/
pets.html

Kennel Software

K9 Bytes
www.k9bytessoftware.com

Kennel Connection
www.kennelconnection.com

Kennel Link
www.kennellink.com

Kennel Soft Atlantis
www.kennelsoft.com

KennelSuite2006
www.planesoftware.com

Marketing Tools

Send Out Cards
www.CustomerContactPlus.com

Pet Care Organizations

National Association of Professional Pet Sitters (NAPPS)
www.petsitters.org

Pet Sitters International (PSI)
www.petsit.com

Small Business Loans

U.S. Small Business Administration (SBA)
www.sba.gov

Small Business Start-Up

About.com
http://sbinformation.about.com

Entrepreneur
www.entrepreneur.com

Service Corps of Retired Executives (SCORE)
www.score.org

Index

Acknowledgments

I would like to thank all of the people who helped and believed in me to launch my career as a successful dog day care owner, as well as realize my dream. A special thank you to my dedicated staff who were as persistent as I in getting the doors open. Also thank you to the great clientele who were so patient while we worked out the kinks. Thank you to Chris Murphy for all of your consulting advice before I became a dog care entrepreneur. It was a long and challenging decision, but the rewards–personally, professionally, and financially–were clearly worth the effort. I would also like to offer a special thank you to my editor, Gordon Mathieson, for all of his hard work and encouragement along the way. This would not have ever come to fruition without you.

About the Author

Darlene Niemeyer has been a dog care provider for many years and has been certified by the National Association of Professional Pet Sitters (NAPPS). After years of corporate jobs, she followed her dream and opened the first dog day care center in Cape Cod, Massachusetts. In 2006, she began a consulting service providing help to others wanting to open a dog-related business. Darlene resides in Naples, Florida where she is successfully running Prima Donna Doggie Pet Sitting Services. You can visit her at www.PrimaDonnaDoggie.com

Photo Credits

Jean M. Fogle @ jeanmfogle.com: 65, 67, 69, 70, 73, 114, 116, 117, 118, 119, 173
Isabelle Francais: 105
Darlene Neimeyer: 56, 73, 136, 206

Shutterstock:
aist1974: 88
Alexander K. Khromtsov: 52
Aleksander Bochenek: 142
Alexey Stiop: 154
Andi Berger: 86
AnnaIA: 20
Annette: 78, 102
Artur Zinatullin: 14
Cate Frost: 95
Cen: 84, 171
Chiran Vlad: 34
christopher nagy: 35
Dainis Derics: 32
Diego Cervo: 27

Dmitry Kramar: 131
Doreen Salcher: 81
ELEN: 156
Elliot Westacott: 162
Eric Isselee: 8-9, 10, 49, 122, 123
Erik Lam: 1
Goldminer: 138
Grahm Prentice: 25
Greg Cerenzio: 120
Hannamariah: 124
HelleM: 186
H Tuller: 19
Ivonne Wierink
Jaime Duplass: 4
Jean Frooms: 71
Jim Vallee: 82
jg1247: 158
John S. Stondilias: 134
Jonathan Pais: 128
Joy Brown: 126
Judy Ben Joud: 90
Justyna Furmanczyk: 169
Kerioak – Christine Nichols: 45
Krzysztof Gorski: 150
Lisa F. Young: 60, 176
Losevsky Pavel: 182
Lucian Coman: 110
Mark Winfrey: 31
Michael Ledray: 42, 170
mlorenz: 152
Monkey Business Images: 97
Multiart: 94
Objectif MC: 75
Okssi: 15
Olga Osa: 58
Pierdelune: 18
Rachel Griffith: 147
Remus: 92

REPPIFOTO: 132
Robert J Daveant: 183
Sally Wallis: 36
Sarah Samela: 38
Sharon Hay: 180
Simon Krzic: 40
Sklep Spozywczy: 144
Silvia Bogdarski: 164
Smart foto: 66
Somer McCain: 76
Ssuaphotos: 100
Studio Newmarket: 135
takedo: 96
The Supe87: 17
Tim Eliott: 89
Tina Rencelj: 33
Tomasz Markowski: 140
Utekhina Anna: 13
Vnlit: 130
Vitcom Photo: 112
Waldemar Dabroski: 22
Willee Cole: 74
william casey: 46
Wolfgang Zintl: 55
Yury Gayvoronskiy: 145
ZQFotography: 166

Logo designs on pages 43, 106, 107, 109, 136, 160, 174 created by Mary Ann Kahn; illustrations by Nebojsa I, Okhitina Tatyana, Stephen Finn

Front cover: Erik Lam, Shutterstock (top and middle); Galina Barskaya, Shutterstock (bottom)
Back Cover: Eric Isselee, Shutterstock

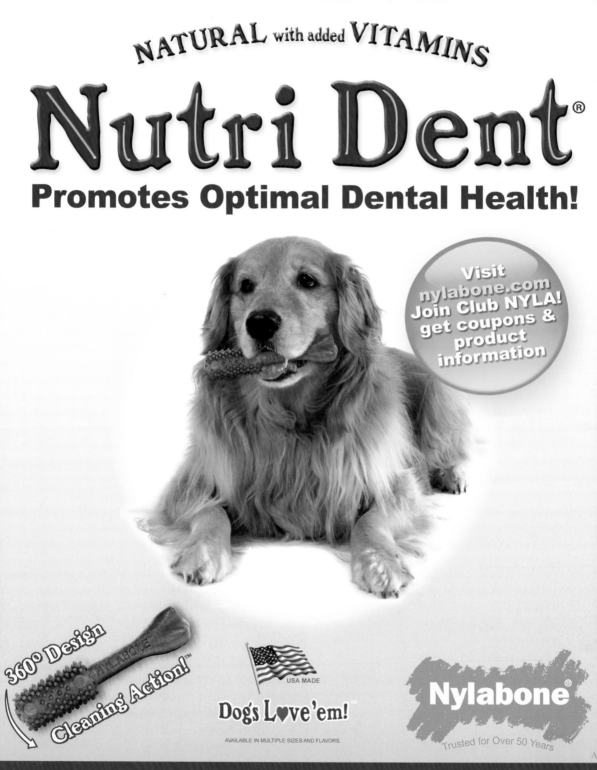